THEORIES: SIZE 14

Laugh!
You know you need to.

Jody Dyer

Crippled Beagle PUBLISHING

Copyright ©2019 Crippled Beagle Publishing
Knoxville, Tennessee

Cover design and artwork by Mary Balas, Bullfrog Graphix
Photo credits: Jody Dyer

Scriptures marked KJV are taken from the KING JAMES VERSION (KJV): KING JAMES VERSION, public domain.
Scriptures marked NIV are taken from the NEW INTERNATIONAL VERSION (NIV): Scripture taken from THE HOLY BIBLE, NEW INTERNATIONAL VERSION ®. Copyright© 1973, 1978, 1984, 2011 by Biblica, Inc.™. Used by permission of Zondervan

ISBN-13: 9781970037265

For interviews or to book speaking engagements, contact the author. dyer.cbpublishing@gmail.com

Dedicated to Suzanne, Judy, Dixie, and Donna

Theories

Beloved reader, I begin this book with Theory 21 because its predecessor, *Theories: Size 12, Laugh! You know you want to,* contains Theories 1-20. In both books, I sometimes allude to highly specific content that may baffle you, as in *What in the world does a mammogram have to do with the song "Bali Hai?"* I write for a wide audience, but I always remember specific readers. Some lines are written, literally, for an audience of one person. In these pages, you will meet all kinds of people: relatives, friends, former coworkers, enemies, and a variety of combatants. I nickname most of my friends in real life and all of my "charcters" here because I need good old plausible deniability. My work is available on Amazon.com, Kindle, Barnesandnoble.com, and in a variety of retail stores. If you don't see my books on shelves, ask store managers to order them. You can certainly contact me directly, but bear in mind that I do not reply to hate mail, even if it comes wrapped in a Mary Kay lip kit.

Chapter titles in *Size 12*:
1: People write diaries hoping someone else will read them.
2: Anyone can learn from anyone.
3: Teachers are the most entertaining people on the planet.
4: The only thing worse than teacher fashion is substitute teacher fashion.
5: You should be nice to everyone you meet because you will meet again, especially if you weren't nice in the first place.
6: Don't judge a woman by her accent or her breast size.
7: Play a sport. Even if you suck at it.
8: If you want the ultimate college experience, join the band.
9: Everyone should work in a restaurant.
10: In youth sports, parents are the real performers.
11: The more a zoo advertises a critter, the less likely visitors are to actually see that critter.
12: Bicycle guys are selfish & make other people late for work.
13: As people get old, they morph into the opposite sex.
14: Humans try to force things to be what things cannot be.
15: Tailgate etiquette is not an oxymoron.

16: Think you can do somebody else's job? Wrong, chicken lips!

17: Funerals beat weddings, for guests anyway.

18: Blind dates are the best dates ever!

19: All mothers need sister wives.

20: Never call a woman fat, lazy, or selfish. Them's fightin' words.

"Don't leave your feet on defense!" —BBJ

Theory 21: All bumper stickers offend someone, but that's the point, right?

Back when I worked for the man, I commuted 45 minutes to an hour every weekday morning and every weekday afternoon. The route from my house to my office was only 21 miles, but the drivers in between slooooooowed meeeeeee dooooooooown. The worst sections where were I cautiously navigated Gnome's and Sharky's school drop-off lines. At that time, Sharky went to a private Catholic school, so there was a low teacher-student ratio but a high child-car ratio. I practiced deep breathing as cars delivered multiples. Gnome attended (still attends) a public school, which is perched in a university and medical community. The car line is long, the cars are long, and most cars deliver only one or two children because these highly educated, successful parents waited a long time to start families.

I was a misfit at both schools. I was a secondarily infertile protestant at Sharky's Catholic institution. I'm a hillbilly in Gnome's swanky school zone zip code many call *The 9-1-9*. I like to think I coined the zip code label, but my cousin Bags also thought she invented hearing aids when she was eight, which she didn't, so I am not claiming *The 9-1-9*; however, I do take credit for making *The 9-1-9* tag micro-locally famous. I should be sharing in merchandizing profits.

The 9-1-9 community is a funky combo of academic tree-huggers and monogrammers. Many 9-1-9 parents walk their children to school, so I study them as I slog the narrow, picturesque drop-off zone. The tree huggers' children dress plainly and don't bother to match. I dig that. Their boys have long hair. Millennials, buzz your boys, for their sakes. Human nature causes teachers to typecast students as they first enter the classroom. I know. I was raised by educators and was one myself for years. Hair is crucial. Is it bad that I told Sharky's first grade class that when I became parent reader, I was also going to be parent barber? I say this in all kindness: When your male child shows up the first day of school with long shaggy hair, his teachers think, *no discipline in that home* and *lice*.

The tree huggers carry coffee mugs, likely filled with organic free-trade stuff. Why do liberals act so guilty all the time? They also walk their dogs. It's bad enough that workin' folks have to wait for you to coddle and chat your way down sidewalks, through crossing guard stations, and all the way to the school's front door. Should we also have to put up with your pets?

Mini-Theory: When you bring your animal to a public place, *you* are seeking attention.

Mini-Theory: *You* are the only person who is interested in your pet. And your dream from the night before. And your wedding.

The monogrammers' girls are all decked out in bright Lily Pulitzer outfits and Matilda Jane ruffle suits. Their boys sport soccer bob haircuts (still too long) and name brand athletic attire. Monogrammer dads wear suits and ties and obviously run the show at work because they apparently don't have to be at work before 8:00 a.m. The mothers wear workout clothes and carry real coffee mugs because they obviously *don't* have to be anywhere and *do* have time to exercise. Must be nice. I tried to take a real coffee mug in the car, but it got wedged under the gas pedal and I almost hit a labradoodle. It's a good thing that lady in a tennis skirt jerked her dog leash. I love my pottery.

I HAVE TO WORK! Well, I may come across kind of mean and hypocritical saying this since I do work from home now, but throughout most of Sharky and Gnome's school years, I have had to hustle to buildings a county away. Now, as a business owner and writer who is most alert and prolific in the early hours, the drop-off drama still overcooks my grits. Maybe I have survivor's guilt. Maybe I am just too busy for your precious morning nonsense.

Of course, if you read *Theories: Size 12,* you know all about my angst with Bicycle Guy, a super fit dude who risks his life for hard thighs while selfishly making other people late for work. Since I published my diatribe ripping him from West to East, there mysteriously and coincidentally appeared two new signs on the short elementary school route. The signs read, "3 feet. It's the law" and "Share the road." Could I be approaching my very first law suit? If he can afford that $10,000, ten-pound bike, I'm in trouble. Let me just say this now to anyone who even thinks about suing me over an anecdote, a nickname, whatever. It's pointless. Let's settle. Would you like my worthless clarinet, which I have forgotten how to play, or would you prefer my husband Tall Child's leaf blower?

Yes, I do say bad things to these people within the confines of my "new" car, Smoke Chow, a Toyota Highlander that cost half what Bicycle Guy paid for his ride and has one quarter of a million miles thus far. I named her Smoke Chow because the previous owner obviously chain-smoked her way around Knox County, Tennessee, with a long-haired white dog who rubbed his body against every square inch of the vehicle. My beloved Big Red, a sixteen-year-old GMC Jimmy, finally snapped her last belt and pretty much birthed her engine in Gnome's school parking lot. I traded Big Red in to my dear neighbor Rock Star's car lot and asked him to find me a new car. He asked, "Do you want to come to the lot and shop around?"

I answered, "With my budget? That would be depressing. Just bring something home. Must haves are heat, air, four doors, and a radio."

He towed Big Red to his lot and brought home Smoke Chow. He loves my children. I trust him. I like Smoke Chow. Once I removed her ashtray and vacuumed the nicotine and dog hair out of the ceiling, we got along just fine.

Back to the arduous drive to school. As my broker friend Iron Man says, "I eat what I kill." My *time* is precious. I need to get back to my writing cave and KILL so I can EAT. To be most efficient, I study humans while I'm trapped in idle. I take notes and use what I see. Beware. No one is safe, especially when I'm hungry. I resort to observing humanity because talking on the phone is illegal (Smoke Chow doesn't have a loudspeaker thingy), and I can't text and drive. I'm a one-finger texter. Plus, a Knox County sheriff's deputy and I had a conversation about texting years ago when I almost side-swiped him on Asheville Highway.

Mini-Theory: When pulled over, teachers should always work the fact that they are teachers into conversations with the police. Teachers—popo—simpatico.

So, as I slowly grind Smoke Chow's wheels behind hundreds of families, I lecture, complain, vent, etc., so Gnome (9) and Sharky learn from Tall Child's and my mistakes. Usually, Sharky (17) drives Tall Child's old car but when it's out of gas, which is often, he rides along with Gnome and me and begs for Chick-Fil-A before drop off. When I feel spiritual, I teach my children Baptist gospel hymns and Lynyrd Skynyrd songs. Right now, we're reviewing The Ten Commandments and studying "Simple Man." But, our favorite time-killing family fun is to discuss bumper stickers. Imagine the dialogue between an eleventh grader, a third grader, and their 45-year-old mama as they theorize why drivers stick certain phrases on their tail ends.

Back when I was a teacher, my buds Scone-Ad (the nutrition teacher), Red Hot Backspace (my computer applications colleague), Man of Measure (the shop teacher), and I had a little in-service lunch time to kill. I brought up bumper stickers. Scone-Ad suggested I write about them. Scone-Ad has perfected the shape, size, texture, and flavor of sausage balls. She also has a unique technique for warming buns in her four-person pop-up camper. Who says home economics is a dead subject? I took notes as my lunch bunch blurted out a list of bumper stickers they love to hate. Then I polled my Facebook friends for their commentary. As I wrote in *Theories: Size 12*, "Anyone can learn from anyone." Let's learn from bumper decals. Be Socratic. Consider the opposing viewpoint for a time before you seek to become offended.

Mini-Theory: If you stick it, will you stick up for it out loud? Or is the sticker your way of making a statement without saying a word?

What statements are *your* bumper stickers making? Current popular phrases in education include "informational text" and "constructed response." Bumper stickers are informational text. Enjoy my list and my buddies' constructed responses.

When Sharky was about five, he breathed into a clean, soft bath towel right out of our dryer and said, "Oooh, this smells just like daddy's friend!" Thus, the nickname for Tall Child's then coworker Febreze, who sports starched shirts, a twelve-month tan, and age-defying hair. He takes excellent care of himself but is a busy guy. Febreze doesn't like the 26.2/13.1 stickers. He said, "Okay, so you are in better shape than I am. Fine, but I don't need the reminder while I am driving around town." Fat thighs matter.

True, true, Febreze. I opened a pedometer in a dirty Santa exchange and wanted to cry. Eventually, thankfully, I unloaded it for a Texas Roadhouse gift card. It's obvious I don't run any 13.1, 26.2, 1.1, or any other number-dot-decimal combo. If you read "Theory 7: Play a sport. Even if you suck at it." you'll understand why my high school track coach nicknamed me Slo-Jo.

"To thine own self be true." —Shakespeare

Marathon and half-marathon runners, what exactly is your point? Females, were you jipped in a non-Title IX school, and now that you are free from male bondage want to let the world know? My big ole' mama Delicious understands. She was born to a Division One basketball player and his all-state wife and grew up with two Division One basketball brothers, but back in the early 1960s, her huge city high school offered nothing but intra-murals for women. She knows basketball and could have been a standout. Ask the score table ladies at Webb School of Knoxville, Tennessee.

Sharky's middle school basketball team, the Eagles, played a Christmas tournament barn-burner against the most expensive private school in town: the Webb Spartans. Webb School's first offense, per Delicious, was that there was no popcorn. Actually, there was NO concessions stand. "These people are terrible hosts," she quipped.

The second offense? The score table ladies changed the possession arrow EVERY time the ball changed teams. Defensive rebound, change, turnover, change, score, change, score, change, defensive rebound, change. You get the picture. Sharky battled the talented Webb Spartans for three quarters, fighting to within two points, all while Delicious focused on the score table ladies and repeatedly yelled, "Stop changing the possession arrow!" By the fourth quarter, she'd had enough. She said, "Help me down."

I said, "Oh, this will be GREAT!"

Mamas, little brothers, grandparents, and fans parted so my 70-year-old mama could climb sideways, left foot first, down the steep bleachers. Ten or so minutes later, I watched in amusement as she did a marching band-worthy flip turn in front of the stands and strutted along the wall behind the basketball goal. She marched to the other side of the gym where her antics were on full display. You see, all the bleachers were on my side of the gym and only the teams' benches and the score table were on the other. Delicious had to scoot sideways behind our team's bench to reach her target. Also, her bright red and green blouse, Christmas reading glasses, Rudolph necklace, and swishing Christmas bell chandelier earrings didn't exactly play down her exhibition. Delicious sucked in and slid behind our coach and said directly to the ladies, who also donned reading glasses, "You have to stop changing the possession arrow every time the ball changes hands. You are affecting the outcome of the ballgame."

Without looking up, one of the women lifted her right hand and made the shoo-shoo motion to Delicious. The lady said, "I don't have time for you."

Delicious said, "Well, you two don't know what the hell you are doing!"

They ignored her. We won in overtime despite the arrow-flipping morons. That week, Sharky's athletic director got a call about the incident from Webb's principal. I told Delicious, who said, "Well, I hope our AD shamed the Webb guy. Did our AD also tell him they had no popcorn?"

Okay, back to the marathon stickers. Are you born-again chunksters so astonished that you graduated from Nutrisystem

University and can survive jogging 26.2 without stroking out that you must tell the world, one driver at a time? Kudo bars to you! Also, why do you use the metric system? To trick people into thinking you ran longer than you actually did? This is America! We count by twelves!

Maybe you're trying to attract another runner. Oh, but what if you marry that other runner, he keeps running, you get pregnant and get fat and can't run anymore? Will you remove the sticker? Maybe you could cross it out and put this one in its place:

Febreze said he did smile and feel better when he saw a sticker that read "0.0."

My old University of Tennessee (UT) Pride of the Southland Band director, The Legend, despised seeing his students run. He would yell through his amplified bullhorn, "Do not run. It is undignified." I get it. When you see an adult running in public, he or she looks awkward, and you sense an emergency.

No joke, though, running a half or full marathon *is* an accomplishment. My cousins Fuzz, Rosco, and Six Shooter and my friend Certified Genius ran the Knoxville Marathon a few years back. Intrigued and impressed, I decided to tailgate on the route. My dear friend Elaine (nicknamed for her dance moves like character Elaine's in *Seinfeld*) lives on a part of the route. I bundled up then baby Gnome, and we sat in Elaine's yard that cold morning to cheer on the runners. Like all good tailgaters, we had food and drink: Krispy Kreme donuts and mimosas.

Runner 3492 partakes.

When I see The 9-1-9's favorite runner, Gazelle, I admire her strong femininity and wonder, *What must it be like to pull anything out of one's closet and drape it over a fit body? She must be comfortable <u>all the time</u>.* Gazelle talked Sharky into running the mile at his fifth-grade field day. He's a basketball player and knew nothing about long-distance running. He burst off the starting line and sprinted. For two miles. He led. For two miles. Then, another boy passed him 25 yards from the finish line. Sharky crossed in second place, ran into the bushes, and threw up. That was his last race.

Running is hard. When I try, it hurts and I hear noises. I guess if you do accomplish such a monumental and exhausting task, you earn a braggy bumper sticker.

I wouldn't mind having some of those endorphins runners talk about. Maybe if I got a dose of them every day, I wouldn't need the Wellbutrin. Well, generic Wellbutrin Bupropion XL. Even my prescription is an *XL*. Ugh. As I type this, I feel two, possibly three stomach rolls fighting for space under my pajama top. Maybe I should run. If I ever do complete a marathon, I will dang sure slap a sticker on Smoke Chow. Speaking of braggy bumpers, what do you think of this old standby?

Proud Parent Of An
HONOR ROLL STUDENT

Let's analyze. First, congratulations on having a child who makes good grades. If not, consider that you may indeed be teaching your child to boast. Let me get religious on you. One of my favorite Bible verses reads, "And whosoever shall exalt himself shall be abased; and he that shall humble himself shall be exalted." Matthew 23:12 (KJV)

In other words, don't over exalt yourself because we all know you are sneakily bragging that you are smart and passed your smart genes down. Your child will be humbled, and so will you.

Quick question: Did your child sail through homework, quizzes, and unit exams for years, then get capsized by the rogue wave of Common Core standards? Hey, it happens. One day, you're cruising down Kingston Pike sporting your honor roll bumper sticker. One superintendent later, you're cruising down Kingston Pike to register Junior for Sylvan Learning Center. Perhaps you should replace the honor roll sticker with something more honest, like:

My child repeated first grade. I blamed it on his hearing problems, but really I didn't read to him twenty minutes a night like I was supposed to. It's all my fault.

What if we come up with hyper-accurate bumper stickers?

> **My child has average grades, and sometimes I yell at him to finish assignments. And sometimes I do the assignments for him because he is sleepy and I am tired of yelling. And I probably yell because I'm drinking. But my child is good at mixing margaritas. That counts for something.**

> **When I got married, I watered down the gene pool. You can't help who you love.**

Delicious's cousin Perd was the most Southern person I've ever known. *Perd* is short for the nickname Perdy, which is a Hogansville, Georgia, pronunciation of the word *pretty*. She was a looker. Perd delivered unique Southern wit with a confident, extended drawl. Her daughter routinely stirred things up in high school and made terrible grades. The principal brought Perd in for a meeting. He said, "Perd, [daughter] is failing and she acts awful."

Perd said, "Well, she may get in trouble and flunk every class, but she's the best damn-looking girl you've EVER had at this school!" New sticker:

> **Intelligence is a gift but being attractive gets you farther in life.**

So does being tough.

Parent, what's your goal with this one? Is this where that whole obsessive bully trend originated? Also, what if your child actually tries to beat up an honor student and gets the stuffing beat out of him? Then what have you got? A weak dummy? Paste cautiously.

As my grandfather, Big Man, would say if his six-foot-five-inch sons whined, "The only thing worse than a sissy is a *big* sissy."

Contrary to my contrarian statement, some students should be recognized for athletic prowess and kinesthetic excellence! Read all about it in "Theory 38: Modern education ruined field day."

My buddy Elaine is as articulate as she is flexible. She summed it up, "Personally, I love the 'my kid beat up your honor student.' I sported it and an 'I /break for boiled peanuts' for several years. I detest the braggy parent bumper stickers 'my kid is an honor student/cheerleader/nuclear physicist/one-legged belly dancer.' My kids are great too, but they don't need me, as their parent, to advertise that fact on the butt of my car. Hopefully, they can get their validation in some better venue than a dirty piece of adhesive vinyl."

Amen, sister wife! By the way, her children are honors students. And black belts.

All I can say is that Obama's tax increase decreased Tall Child's paycheck significantly, which decreased my quality of life by lowering my grocery budget. Geez. I did qualify for a student loan for my master's degree during his term, though. Yippee! I took my boys to Hilton Head. Huh? What? Who *said* that?

Why do folks leave campaign bumper stickers on their cars long after elections decide winners? To gloat? To pout? New sticker:

> **Vote for the candidate who will raise my grocery budget, grant giant student loans, then forgive said student loans. Beach or bust!**

I guess I won't see the ocean again unless I pursue a Ph.D.

Besides reminding me of the snake in my silverware drawer, this rattles of militia. It is historical, but it's still eerie. The King of Kodak, my loving, liberal, witty geography teacher who diagnosed me with slow-twitch muscle fibers, says this sticker "insults our founding fathers." The imagery comes from a cartoon Benjamin Franklin created to suggest colonists send rattlesnakes to England since England sent criminals to the colonies. Rumor is those bad boys settled in Georgia, my home state. Marines, Tea Party conservatives, and, well, rednecks fly it and stick it. Some say it's racist; some say it's patriotic. Tall Child says it reminds him of all the "Mr. No-Shoulders" sliding through the grass waiting to fang him. I like it.

Good idea. I bet your child is on the honor roll. New sticker:

> **I break for anything that outweighs me and whose physical properties can kill me before I sling my next boiled peanut hull out of the car window.**

It's too bad bicycle guys don't have room for bumper stickers. What would those stickers say?

> **Big Traffic Baby On Board.**

My colorful neighbor and surrogate grandmama to Sharky and Gnome, Auntie Mame, said, "I saw a car with 'Practice random acts of kindness' on the bumper, all while the driver was honking at someone, riding his bumper, and shooting a bird!" New sticker:

 , but hypocrites suck more. See driver.

Is it bad that sometimes I love shooting birds? Is that because I grew up in Pigeon Forge, I fished with dough balls, and my crushes wore acid wash jeans with Members Only jackets? When I taught ninth grade, I used a table for my desk and draped a hideous Dollar Tree tablecloth over it. Why? Well, when knucklehead students visited the wall-mounted hand sanitizer for the fourteenth time and asked, "Hey, are you going to make us work today?" I could answer with polite patience while sliding my hand under the table to flip the bird. It helped.

Don't tell me how to live. I Googled this one.

C is the symbol for Islam
O is the symbol for peace
E is the symbol for males/females
X is the symbol for Judaism
I is dotted with a Wicca pentacle
S is the symbol for the yin-yang or Confucianism
T is the symbol for Christianity

Wicca? Really? REALLY? Why'd they leave out good old Buddha and the cannibals? One afternoon as I rode shotgun in my mother-in-law Bop's Cadillac, she said, "I like that sticker. It's nice." She likes the idea of people getting along, but I seriously doubt she's a fan of the Wicca pentacle.

Think about it this way. There is no choice. If you exist, you coexist. As a banker, I worked with the public; I watched rich, educated people coexist with farmers, opioid addicts, customers with online banking *and* dementia, the coffee service guy, the FedEx guy, college students, and sovereign citizens who "don't want no debit card." It was like an East Tennessee, PG-13 version of Sesame Street. So yes, if you live, you coexist. Well, until natural selection weeds your substandard non-honor roll family out of existence.

Meh. The evolutionists try so hard, always working their way into public schools to expel God and take over science curriculum. It's a shame. I'm gonna pray for y'all. Science and faith coexist. Read *Mere Christianity* by the superb C.S. Lewis. New sticker:

> **I am trying to look like a science stud by displaying this Darwin fish, but if I ever get deathly ill or go to jail, I'll switch my sticker.**

Beep! Beep! My uncle Trout often explains his religious philosophy to non-believers like this: "You might as well believe, because if you don't, you'll go straight to hell." Little Linda told me she does love Jesus whether or not she honks or re-posts on Facebook. She added, "Jesus knows I love him, and I don't think He likes social media."

I taught boys and girls who had NEVER been on vacations. I wondered if they knew what HHI, 30A, PCB, and so on meant. You know, from a distance at a certain speed, HHI looks kind of like HIV. Careful. New sticker:

You can go anywhere if you finish school, get a decent job, save your money, maintain your health, and have a little good luck. OR, you could master the FAFSA and hit the road. Whooooop!

I am guilty. Please don't honk at me when the light turns red. Um, I'm on a call, okay. Working mothers must multi-task and often, during the solitude of a car ride is the ONLY time a woman can make appointments, talk with friends, or negotiate with the IRS without interruption from a child or a man. I think all mothers should get to be happy ghosts after they die so they can watch their widowers try to call doctors, insurance agents, pay school lunch fees online, talk to teachers, make excuses to in-laws, you get the picture.

I just flipped through Sharky's history textbook here at home to research this one. It looks like that peace stuff is impossible. New sticker:

Let's not shoot each other *most* of the time.

Here's a sticker that always causes me to slow down and check out the driver:

Do you? Is that why you are pulling out of the Roosters/Hooters/Twin Peaks parking lot at 10:00 p.m.? Let me guess; you brought wifey a doggie bag to show your affection. Oh, and your car is weaving. I bet your wife calls you "hubby" and you two take lots of date night selfies and have a combined Facebook page.

Delicious loves to be interviewed. As we were driving one day, I interviewed her. I asked, "What are your favorite things about my daddy?"

She said, "Well, he's smart and unselfish. And, he's an animal lover."

I was a sophomore, and I had finally figured out what happened during sex (not through personal experience—an upperclassman told me). Anyway, when Delicious said *animal lover,* I said, "Oh my gosh! GROSSSSSSSS! Why would you *tell* me that!?! I can't even look at you!"

She asked, "Bug, what is wrong with you? Pooh has always loved animals."

Relieved, I said, "Oh, thank the Lord. I thought you meant like what they do on 'As the World Turns,' as in *animalistic* lover."

I MISS my Yorkie Buzz, but I don't miss Tall Child's constant complaining about Buzz. New sticker:

I hate my wife's dog.

PREPARING FOR THE ZOMBIE APOCALYPSE

Well, I suppose this one could scare children. Tall Child and I are addicted to "The Walking Dead" and "The Talking Dead." I taught host Chris Hardwick's nephew. Hardwick and I Tweeted each other! Sheep? Melatonin? Nah, when I can't sleep, I imagine myself in the first hour of a zombie apocalypse. If I hear Ebola/bird flu/mad cow on National Public Radio, I get excited and start looking for batteries, my Pampered Chef pizza cutter, and Vienna sausages.

New bride? Preppy? Monied enough to have your clothes stamped? This picture cracks me up because there is no way a monogram belongs on a wife-beater. I guess this is a tank top. Never mind.

I did the math. This is how many three-letter combinations we can make from the English alphabet:

18,331,430,051,209,300,000,000,000

I have no idea if that is correct because I dug the formula out of the recesses of my brain. I think the formula goes 26x25x24 and on down to . . . x 1 = that answer. When I researched online to verify the formula, I became confused. To sum it up (ha), yes, monogram are unique, in a way.

During my bumper sticker research, I got more negative comments about this bumper sticker than any other, hands down. Basically, these stickers imply that couples are happily married, the husband is taller than the wife, he doesn't cheat, he doesn't throw his wife under the bus when in-laws make demands, he has a job, etc. He is so awesome that you represent his image with cute adhesive paper. Oh, and your children. Your *children*. They too decorate the window in descending age and, presumably, height. Look, I taught junior high, so I know for a fact that your thirteen-year-old son is shorter than your eleven-year-old daughter. At least your boys and girls are physically fit and artistic. They all appear to be holding flutes or balls.

What a healthy, happy, normal family. Are you so calm and organized and kind on long road trips to hot Orlando or expensive New York City? And, oh, your sweet little pets are part of the family too. Cute! I bet your mother calls your Border Collie her "granddog." The cats and dogs sit side by side as the happy family takes Sunday drives. Everything is groovy. You COEXIST so well while I keep a switch on the dashboard. Corporal punishment is still legal in the state of Tennessee. Whoa, whoa, softies. No worries! Ask Sharky and Gnome. They will tell you I never follow through on any of my threats.

I suppose mamas and daddies paste these reminders to represent what they are trying hard to be: normal, well-adjusted, loving, and close.

Marriage is such a dynamic adventure with so many variables. What happens if your neighbor shoots your dog? Or steals your husband? How much do these stickers cost? What happens if "I Love My Wife" guy disappoints? Do you keep acetone in the glove compartment?

I see all kinds now: Disney families, zombie families (YES!), and even pirate families. While writing this I felt left out of the fun, so I created a custom sticker for my clan:

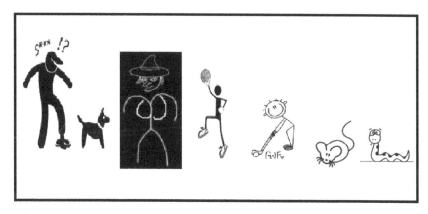

The mouse was a frequent visitor. Let's hope the snake was in the silverware drawer only once to catch the mouse and move on.

The last bumper sticker Big Red wore was a blue oval boasting the name of Sharky's elementary school. That was back in 2011 when I taught at a "rough" middle school. One day, while I desperately tried to teach pre-algebra to a bunch of non-interested eighth graders, my sticker disappeared. Along with my tail lights.

Of all the commentary I've provoked and received regarding this topic, my favorite response came from my dear friend, tie dye artist, and vacation Bible school aficionado, Flower Child. She wrote, "I love bumper stickers! I don't agree with all of them, but I love to see the super different opinions of everyone!!! Makes the world go 'round."

As my husband said not long ago, "If you can't get along with Flower Child, there's something wrong with you."

**I BRAKE FOR YOU,
FLOWER CHILD.**

I BRAKE FOR YOU.

Theory 22: Wedding vows need translation.

When we girls get engaged, it seems as though everyone we know is compelled to toss out tidbits of unsolicited advice. Many brides-to-be happily float in a fog of relief and romance, and they often buck when they hear negative comments about marriage. We become moody, obsessed with detail, or, in my case, nervous wrecks. Perhaps this is why some of us morph into "bridezillas" or show up to the ceremony tottering three sheets to the wind. Perhaps some brides obsess over colors of tablecloths, candle heights, stamped paper napkins, chair covers, and rice vs. bird seed because they tie the success of the *marriage* to the success of the *wedding*. Depending on your age and marital status, you have either been exposed to or are now generating cringe-inducing sentences that begin with:

"Well, when *I* got married . . . "
"If I were you . . . "
"If I could do it all over again . . . "
"Whatever you do, don't . . . "
"Make sure you . . . "
"You'd better . . . "

The bride may feel like a Ritz cracker on the beach, surrounded by sea gulls harping for personal need, comfort, and attention. The comments, warning of inevitable hardships to come, flare through the fog. Hey, marriage is good. Of all the advice I have heard or read, two pieces stand out and remain true. The first came from my mother-in-law Bop. She warned, "If you don't want to do something the rest of your life, don't ever do it. If you don't want to take the garbage down to the bottom of the driveway every Monday, don't EVER do it. Ever." Why? Why did I cut those shrubs back twelve years ago? WHY???????

The other advice that probably best saves my and Tall Child's union is from *The Holy Bible*. In the book of Matthew, Peter asks Jesus, "Lord, how often shall my brother sin against me, and I forgive him? Up to seven times?" Jesus said, "I do not say to you, up to seven times, but up to seventy times seven." I've internalized most of the Bible verses I use in daily life, so the words may not be exact. I have to dumb things down for myself. Verses in this book may be written as combinations of my two favorite versions of the Bible. The writer in me prefers the King James version, but the sinner in me needs the easier to understand New International Version.

Tall Child, again, I'm sorry I backed your car into a palm tree at Alvin's Island in Panama City Beach. It's immature to slam doors. I apologize for my quick temper. It is ridiculous of me to throw things at you. I'm sorry that I act more like an opponent than a teammate, but just think, all those years of college basketball prepared you for marriage. Rebound!

I'm no relationship expert, but I do know this after being married almost twenty years. When you stand at the altar, you may think you have it all figured out and you've made a safe, solid choice, but you are beginning a journey that has no itinerary, no guarantees, and no real predictability, other than the human and statistical fact that vows articulate what is *likely* to happen. Listen.

Tall Child should have been properly warned. I should have realized then that my marriage would be completely different from my parents' marriage because Tall Child and I are, duh, different than my parents.

Who said "Comparison is the thief of joy?" You and your spouse are a two-person family unit. You are a unique creation. Don't compare, but do OVER-communicate, especially on the front end. You preachers need to help us out a little here. Traditional wedding vows are beautiful and certainly a poetic way to hop onto the love boat. But the pretty words aren't direct or descriptive. We sacrifice realistic for optimistic. Why can't we have both? I got this idea when I watched my friend Fancy, who is a master at American Sign Language, "sign-sing" me a country song. I love to sit on her screened porch, drink boxed wine, and watch her translate the words of country ballads from her Spotify playlist into physical form. Her multi-dimensional abilities in expression inspired me. Sometimes, we need a different approach to communicate the essence of words. Here, I translate the ceremony and vows. Perhaps this book and its first volume could be wedding gifts for unsuspecting love birds. Maybe Fancy can sign all this and take it to the next level.

Friends, all we need is a translator up there beside the preacher, just like the sign language lady who stands beside the TV evangelist, except that when the preacher says his line, the translator states his aloud for all to understand. If the bride or groom is hearing impaired, hire Fancy. Enjoy my translations.

CEREMONY

Preacher: *Dearly beloved, we are gathered here in the presence of God to join this man and this woman in holy matrimony.*

Translator: Audience member, you may want to be here or you may be mad because it's a football Saturday, and you have already spent an entire paycheck on this couple, but they love you, or at least they felt obligated to include you, so suck it up. There's an open bar at the reception. This is a church so behave and understand that God is here and you need to sit there and think about your own marriage and pray for this one that's about to start. If your spouse glares at you, smile and squeeze her hand. If she winces, kiss her on the cheek. If she looks at you lovingly, do the same and pat yourself on the back.

Preacher: *Marriage is ordained by God, regulated by God's commandments, blessed by our Lord Jesus Christ, and to be held in honor among all people.*

Translator: Bride and groom, if you want a successful marriage, don't listen to what your friends and family say. There is a rule book. It's called The Holy Bible. Happy hour is singular, just like you'll be if you stay more than one happy hour more than once a week. If the waitress asks, "Do you want another round," you need to think, *What would Jesus do?* Boy, get in your truck and high-tail it home. EVERYONE you know should honor your marriage. Audience, maybe you think she's a nut. Maybe you think he is a control freak. It doesn't matter. A husband or wife should never have to compete with in-laws, friends, or coworkers, within reason, for attention or money or time. Respect the couple. Bride, if your mama is obnoxious, handle it. Groom, if your mama is laying on the guilt trip, deal. No one really knows what goes on in a marriage except the husband and wife.

~~~

When my cousin Bags went to premarital counseling with then fiancé Guitar Hero, the preacher said, "Blood gives bad news to blood." Amen.

Preacher: *Groom/Bride, will you have this person to be your wife/husband? Will you pledge your loyalty, love, and honor, duty, and service, in all faith and tenderness, to live with her/him and cherish her/him according to the ordinances of God?*

Translator: I don't know why I'm asking this because you proposed/accepted, but here goes: Groom/Bride, are you absolutely Danny and Sandy sure? Can you say with all your being, "You're the one that I want?"

No matter how certain you are, you are taking a leap of faith: you really don't know someone until you are married to him for a while.

~~~

For example, a gorgeous grad-school buddy of mine thought she was happily married and raising her children in a wholesome household until one MOTHER'S DAY when she opened the local paper. She scanned the birth announcements and spotted her husband in a picture with his stripper girlfriend and their new baby. Yes, he posed for a photo knowing it would be in the paper and knowing he was married to someone else. I recently ran into her at Gnome's basketball jamboree. She told me the amazing story as her now ex-husband disappointed the family once again by being late to the game with their son's basketball shoes. I don't know which is worse: a husband who fathers a stripper's baby or a husband who neglects basketball gear. It's all about the shoes. Finally, the moron showed up. As he trotted up the bleachers, he tripped and almost faceplanted into the third row. "Poetic justice," I said. "But, dang it, he's all right. I was hoping he would hit the edge of the bleacher and his teeth would cut through his lips."

Living together is daring. Marriage is binding. Consider similar triangles and proportionate ratios (more on that later):

$$\frac{\text{living together}}{\text{boxes}} = \frac{\text{married}}{\text{children}}$$

You can also work the problem this way:

$$\frac{\text{living together}}{\text{married}} = \frac{\text{boxes}}{\text{children}}$$

VOWS

Bride and Groom: *I take you to be my husband/wife, to love and cherish, for richer or for poorer, in joy and sorrow, in sickness and in health, as long as we both shall live.*

Translator: Let's break this one down by terminology. When you say these vows, you say…

Spouse: You take each other every day, regardless of bliss or chaos, because you are partners in bliss and chaos and all misery that spews from the mailbox.

Cherish: Put God first. Then each other. Not work (companies are paper, not souls), not in-laws who want to make your marriage their hobby, not friends who miss their drinking buddies.

~~~

Back in the early '90s, at age nineteen, my friend Goo Goo Cluster drove to Waco, Texas, to rescue two cousins from a cult. He was unsuccessful but escaped personal brainwashing. When he came home a week later, he told fascinating, eerie stories of foot-washing, chanting, and daily routines. I asked why he left so soon. He said, "The first day I got there the leader took all my Boston

Celtics T-shirts from me. He said I made Larry Bird my god. Those people are nuts."

A yoga teacher told me it's okay to squeeze self between God and spouse. Wife, you're not selfish for helping a friend. Husband, you're not selfish for playing golf. You are partners, not employer-employee. To cherish someone is to respect his being, his desires, his dreams. I dream of wearing a size ten, so before I have a few glasses of wine, I walk my neighborhood. Tall Child respects my dream.

Richer: Congratulations for having an emergency savings account. You are in the worldwide minority. What's it like? Be good stewards and set money aside for WHEN, not IF, bad things happen. If only one spouse works, the other should be respectful by not wasting money and not bombarding him/her with demands as soon as he/she walks in the door. Men, if your wife earns more than you, slide your ego to the side and say thanks.

Poorer: Recessions happen. One spouse may be up while the other is down, professionally speaking. Don't let credit bureaus dictate your life. Do make financial decisions together. Do not lie about money. Hide some, though. Whether you are man or wife, spend and save like a single mother.

Joy: Pay attention *during good times.* Delicious says, "The best days are the days when nothing out of the ordinary happens."

Sorrow: If you live long enough, you'll experience tragedy. Brace yourself and your marriage for inevitable heartache. Oh, and follow the Ten Commandments so that you aren't the source of that heartache.

Sickness: Believe it or not, strep throat hurts as terribly for a woman as it does for a man. When one partner is down, the other must step up and shouldn't have to be asked. Notice need.

~~~

I had strep throat on Halloween. Sharky was four-years-old. While I lay on the sofa planning my funeral, he had a candy war with color-coded battalions of Skittle's and M&M's. Dead candy was eaten off the battlefield, a.k.a., the floor.

EXCHANGE OF RINGS

Preacher: *In the giving and receiving of rings, the man and woman give to each other an outward sign of an inward commitment. Let the rings be a sign of your love.*

Translator: "Let the circle be unbroken." Don't. Take. The ring. Off. Why would you? If you take that ring off, other than to comply with work safety standards, you are telling your spouse, "I don't care if people think I am single." It's disrespectful. The ring is a reminder to YOU and to OTHERS that you are committed to someone else.

~~~

Delicious likes to sing on her way to weddings, "With this ring, I do dread, all the [expletive] that lies ahead." Tall Child and I have flaws and we have certainly made hurtful, stupid mistakes. Honestly, we've experienced the extreme ends of almost every vow. I like to tell people who question our relationship, "Everything you have ever heard about Tall Child and me is absolutely true."

Reader, enjoy this list of marital advice my friends and I compiled:

o Keep God in the center of your marriage and you will never go wrong.
o Money doesn't cause problems in marriages. SECRETS about money cause problems in marriages.
o It is cruel to physically reject a spouse, unless he/she is a pervert.
o Be nice when your spouse is fat. There's a good chance she'll be skinny and you'll be fat at some point.
o Don't let your honeymoon be the last trip you take alone together.
o Do not expect to change his or her basic personality.

29

- Make sure one of you travels for work.
- Don't go to bed mad at each other. Let him be right and restart the argument in the morning.
- Give each other space and time to do the things each of you enjoys.
- Never marry someone you wouldn't happily give half of everything you own.
- Stay interested and interesting.
- It's always the man's fault.
- Be willing to concede and/or see your spouse's perspective. If you are obsessed with being right all the time, you're just an a-hole.
- Don't call your mama from Lover's Leap (Tall Child). Gag me with a dead Smurf!
- Hold hands when you argue.
- Even better, argue naked, but not while also using your Fry Daddy.
- Deadline Diva says, "Have separate bedrooms. Everyone needs alone time and privacy. You can visit each other when the need arises." Get it?
- My dear friend Tech Savvy says, "I've heard the first 50 years are the hardest."

I like the advice our former pastor The Confederate gave Tall Child after we had been married about two years. He said, "In matters of right and wrong and big decisions, all you have to remember Tall Child, for the rest of your life, is to defer to Bug."

Hang in there, lovers.

Theory 23: There are right ways and wrong ways to date online.

Username: HogtheBulldog
Age: 56
Hobbies: Hiking, reading Shakespeare aloud, playing jazz piano

In a later chapter, I'll spell out my romantic woes with a man I've never met who used my W-2 and Social Security number to prove our financial bond and make hay with...my tax refunds. While I'm committed to Tall Child and will not allow a stranger or flawed government institution to put us asunder, marriage can be difficult. Some of us just aren't cut out to be roommates with anyone. Circumstances, finances, mid-life hormonal changes, children (yes), and other issues can chip away at the foundation. Maybe I will end up divorced someday. I hope not. But, if I do, I've learned from friends that the modern-day dating scene, which appears to take place on a digital screen, is not for me.

My former teaching colleague Red Hot coauthored this chapter. She's a single mother to Suspenders and Spectacles. While Red Hot makes a fine cougar with her bright auburn curls, eager laugh, vibrant personality, cowboy boots, and stacked degrees, she is an often discouraged member of the dating screen scene. We worked side by side as educators, so I had a first-hand window into her love life. Her keen sense of humor and sharp self-awareness afforded us countless hours of laughter at her online pursuers' and her expenses. We collected dating data from other online love-seekers and compiled them here for those of you who may benefit from a guide.

Educators like a framework for understanding. Red Hot and I constructed the framework for understanding online romance by applying Howard Gardner's *Theory of Multiple Intelligences*. He explains that humans learn in eight styles: visual-spatial, bodily-kinesthetic, logical-mathematical, musical-rhythmic, naturalistic, interpersonal, intrapersonal, and verbal-linguistic. One style dominates the learner's abilities. For example, my dominant Multiple Intelligence is *interpersonal* and I scored a 47 in that category. By comparison, I scored a pitiful 9 in spatial reasoning. It makes sense. I grew up so close to Dollywood I could hear the train whistle and smell funnel cakes, but every time I go to Dollywood, I must use a map and depend on Gnome to help me find a bathroom. Let's break down online dating in hopes of limiting digital disappointment.

VISUAL-SPATIAL LEARNERS: You learn by observation and visual stimulation.

When you set up your profile, be realistic. We are way past Y2K, so if you're wearing a Coca-Cola shirt and leaning against an electric blue Camaro, you're suspect. Guys, it's normal to be bald and less masculine when you're 60. Time changes us. Consult "Theory 13: As people age, they morph into the opposite sex" for explanation. The same goes for Glamour Shots. No one is that soft.

The way I see it, you've got two options. One: Have a professional photographer take a beautiful photo outside at sunset, like the white shirts, khaki shorts, family catering shots on Panama City Beach. Make sure that Jergens Natural Glow is even and ripe. Suck in. As Delicious tells me, "Fluff up your hair." Candids show the real you, your soul, but may not flatter. Every time someone takes a candid of me, I look like the centerfold in *Just Busted*. Two: I DOUBLE-DOG-DARE you. Pose in a swimsuit under fluorescent lights. No Spanx. No lies. How about a five-photo collage of you? I'm thinking grocery store, early morning base make-up only, mid-workout, 5:00 p.m. conference call, and right out of the hairdresser's sink. That's my worst look. Yes, I need to drop some pounds, but really, I think my head is too small for my body, which is why I follow Delicious's command and fluff my hair. Soaking wet, I look like a fat Yorkie. Online, let it all hang out. Be your before-model self and find a person who is attracted to the REAL you.

BODILY-KINESTHETIC LEARNERS: You learn through physical activity and body language. You like hands-on learning and role-playing (gross).

No matter how close you feel in cyberspace, your first face-to-face will feel like a blind date, especially if you misled with a Glamour Shot or a yearbook superlative picture. See "Theory 18: Blind dates are the best dates ever" for encouraging info on setups. The more you embellish online, the more nervous you'll be in person. So, don't over promise for you're sure to under deliver and start things off badly in 3D.

If you type "I'm a Southern lady who loves to dance to the oldies" you'd better be able to down a mint julep and shag to The Tams. What if your date turns out to be a handsome, loafered Grand Strand shag champion and all you know bring are Merlot and the moves of the Electric Slide? He'll run like a scalded haint.

When asked about hobbies, why do people always put "reading and hiking" in the blank? The average American reads ONE book per YEAR. I know; I'm an author. If you live in Mississippi, where the land is flat, you can't hike. That's like saying you're going to climb a trampoline. Seriously, I'm warning you. Do NOT say you like to hike unless you can climb a mountain. I told a cute boy from Seymour, Tennessee, "I just *love* hiking." He asked me to help him chaperone a youth group to The Chimney Tops in The Great Smoky Mountains. Oh, my knees were wobbly, all right. I was breathless, for sure. It was ugly. *I* was ugly. The STEEP 3.3-mile hike has a 901-foot elevation gain per mile and difficulty rating of 6.27. No one should sweat uphill and crawl across boulders on her belly on a first date. It's a good thing we were with a church group; I could pray out loud without judgement.

Be in the here and now. Being physically fit in 1985 does not carry over to 2017. Played basketball in college? Great! How about now? Where do you post up? It looks like some of you "athletic types" post up at the concession stand.

Don't try to be all "I'm a tough football playin' stud" by straight-facing your pictures. That just screams mug shot, or dud, or wife beater, or desperate, or forced into this by a relative, or toothless. We don't believe you are "happy, fun-loving, and adventurous" if you look like you just finished probating a will.

LOGICAL/MATHEMATICAL LEARNERS: You like patterns and processes.

Distance matters. Even online. Do the math. If you live in the WCC or PAC 10, don't promote yourself in the SEC. Why *select* the challenge of a long-distance relationship? While we're on this topic, Red Hot wants to know: Is there a woman shortage in California and Michigan? Every other profile she sees is from a man in California or Michigan. Maybe you are tax-weary and looking for a hideout in the Great Smoky Mountains. I can hear a Michigander saying, "Guys, I'm going to find a nice Tennessee girl and move to one of those warm hollers full of sovereign citizens. No more mall hair. No more snow shovels. No more authority!"

Don't advertise that you love children and then pout when your online, single mother love interest keeps putting you off. Think. She's dating online because, after work, she must do EVERYTHING and has no free time until her children go to bed. She can't talk on the phone. She can't go anywhere to meet men. Nothing is convenient for her. This is your chance to shine! Cater to her schedule. If you go on a date, guy, you should make all the decisions. She likely always comes last, so put her first. Too many women must be conventional men these days. Need more time with that concept? Read "Theory 20: Never call a woman fat, lazy, or selfish. Them's fightin' words."

Know your body. Sync its description with reality, or you will become heart-broken and potentially broke. My sweet, naïve bank customer sat in my office wearing a snug T-shirt and sweatpants and said, "Bug, I'm gettin' married soon as my boyfriend finishes up his service this month." Reader, she's 63 years old, sports a twelve-pound fupa, and her teeth look like The University of Tennessee's football field checkerboard endzone. Her boyfriend, on the other hand, is a 35-year-old bodybuilding, about-to-retire marine. They met online. Three months after her "boyfriend" appeared in Tennessee her Social Security deposit disappeared.

MUSICAL/RHYTHMIC LEARNERS: You love music, and lyrics help you learn. You like vibration and rhythm but not from too many sources. You are sensitive and responsive to sound.

Tell the truth. No one likes jazz. Or opera. Or classical music. Am I wrong? Maybe I'm uncultured. My guess is that at some point in our courtship, I lied to Tall Child and said I liked fancy music. One late afternoon after work when I was around seven months pregnant with Sharky, Tall Child surprised me with tickets to the local symphony. My first thought was, *How am I going to fake excitement?* My second thought was, *How am I going to stay awake?*

He was proud and sweet. I put on a good show. He asked if I wanted to change out of my business casual work clothes. I said, "No. I'm comfortable." Once comfortable, I don't take chances with wardrobe. And, now that I'm a full-time writer, I wear bras only when I have client meetings or leave the house. I'm a *Freedom Writer*! Back to the story….

Tall Child asked, "Should I wear a tie?"
"No, ties aren't required at our symphony." (Are they?)
"You sure?"
"Oh, yes. We're in Knoxville not in Manhattan." (Wit is a helpful diversionary tool.)
"I'll ask Mom. She wants us to stop by their house on the way."
We stopped by my in-laws' house.
Bop wasn't there to check Tall Child's outfit, so she called. She told him to wear a tie. Then she asked to speak with me. "What are you wearing, Bug?"

"A giant work outfit."

"Okay."

I was trying to get him to go tieless so I wasn't underdressed alone. All this is to say that if you boast that you hike and listen to classical music, once your online love goes viral, meaning physical, you may have to hike and listen to classical music. Beware, Beethoven. And buy the right clothes.

Daters, *doo-de-doo* woo with music. Find a song that helps you relate to him/her. You may strike just the right chord. My Baby Boomer Tall Child did. He won my heart on our first few dates by playing the Tams and knowing the words to every song. Plus, he told me he was a great shagger.

My daddy tried out for the Glee Club at J.J. Kelly High School in Wise, Virginia. The director listened and gave Pooh an odd look to which Pooh responded, "Oh, I sound much better in a group." Also, don't say you play guitar. Someone may ask you to play guitar.

NATURALISTIC LEARNERS: You respond to plants and animals and like to classify.

Boys *and* girls, if you type, "I love the great outdoors" and you live in East Tennessee, you'd better know how to pack a beer cooler, carry a rifle, and bait a hook. Hate to be cold? Don't say you're an NRA member who eats wild game unless you're willing to freeze your tail off in a duck blind and gnaw on deer jerky for lunch. For heaven's sake, be careful. What if your first face-to-face date demands physical fitness or exposure to weather?

My cousins A-Boo and Bags and I had this conversation not too long ago:

Bug: *What is your first date nightmare scenario?*

A-Boo: *Scuba diving. I'm not sure I could get a wetsuit up over my thighs. I eat too much cheese.*

Bug: *Any situation requiring a bathing suit.*

Bags: *See-saw.*

Naturalist learners like water, dirt, and outdoor pursuits. Pooh was a naturalist. When I was little, he worked at Chalet Village in Gatlinburg, Tennessee, as a rental manager. His shift ended at 3:30 p.m., but he got home around supper time. Pooh cast his afternoon through fishing holes in Elkmont, Greenbrier, Metcalf Bottoms, and other rocky havens along Little River in The Great Smoky Mountains National Park. Raised by widowed mother Wimmie, he had few available male role models. He taught himself to fish at the Sevier County Public Library. He then taught his friend and coworker Duke how to fly fish during Chalet Village lunch breaks. In the first lesson Pooh chalked a 25-foot diameter circle in the parking lot's empty space, showed Duke how to grip the rod, and demonstrated proper casting technique. As Duke improved his finesse and aim over several weeks' time, Pooh decreased the diameter of the chalk circle more and more. Duke swears that Pooh could cast his hand-tied flies directly into the Chalet Village coffee cups.

As Delicious says, "If you can't fish without help, don't fish. There is nothing more frustrating than watching someone who doesn't know how to bait, cast, and reel, bait, cast, and reel." Pooh was a patient teacher in the natural environment. Delicious? Not so patient a learner. She is NOT a princess, but she DOES like comfort.

On The Crippled Beagle Farm, Mama and Daddy had three gardens. One lay below the chicken pen, where, um, fertilizer worked its way downhill to produce huge Better Boy, Mr. Stripey, and Rutgers tomatoes. Another garden rested parallel to the gravel road. It hosted blue-ribbon, 200-pound pumpkins, yellow squash, and cucumbers. In a more private setting, between a small ridge and Kellum Creek, Pooh and Delicious tended a two-acre garden planted with beans, okra, onions, gourds, and more. Though she appreciates nature and loves cruising The Crippled Beagle Farm and Aunt Joo-Joo's Naked Lady Farm on an ATV, she does so at night. Delicious hates to be hot. She and Pooh were a great match. One day, well, I'll let her tell it.

Extreme heat separates the men from the boys when it comes to gardening. It was July-hot and Pooh and I intended to hoe out all the weeds in the two-acre garden. I wore an old cotton sundress, bra, granny panties, socks, tennis shoes, and a Georgia visor. Pooh had on a worn-thin gray T-shirt, cotton shorts, white socks, tennis shoes, and an Atlanta Braves baseball hat. The sun was unbearable. My eyes stung from the river of sweat flowing down from my pudgy face into my 44DDD bra. My nylon underpants stuck to me like slugs stick to an empty dog pan on a humid summer night. Lo and behold, I looked over at Pooh, and he had taken off his shirt.

Oh, no, buddy! Not in my presence. Neither baby, boy, nor man goes bare-chested in my family unless he is in *a swimming pool. I ordered, "Put that shirt back on." He ignored. I thought* Okay, I'll show him!

I took of the dress, the bra, and the panties, and kept on only the visor, socks, and shoes. There I was with V-shaped, sweaty, fat, flopping boobs, cellulite dimpled thighs, and a snow white oversized stomach for all of nature to observe. Ahhh...revenge....

Pooh, still focused on his hoeing, didn't even look up. I got mad. I began to hoe at a frantic pace, a pace which undoubtedly shook the ground as I raised the hoe as high as I could before I chopped down, seeking Pooh's peripheral vision.

Pooh finally *looked up, took in the image, all 200 plus pounds of lard, and admonished in his usual, low, calm voice, "Mr. Terry is going to see you." (Mr. Terry was 84 years-old and two rectangular acres away.)*

Did Pooh laugh? Oh, yes!

INTERPERSONAL LEARNERS: You are intuitive to the needs, thoughts, and emotions of others. You navigate well among different personality types.

These learners are heavy thinkers and superb communicators. You see them in the real world as teachers, religious leaders, mediators, psychologists, waiters, and actors. They detect B.S. immediately. They can take it and dish it out.

While interpersonal learners are excellent mind-readers, they tire of the process. My buddy Agape Agave says, "It's not work that wears us out, it's all the social gymnastics we have to perform with our coworkers." Amen!

If you take a liking to an interpersonal learner, wow him or her with direct communication. Red Hot explains, "Don't send a flirt, smile, or any other random one-click response. Send me a message with real words. If I take the time to email you, respond—even if only to say 'Thanks, but no thanks.'"

Whoa, boy, do be careful with the text messages. Remember that texts and emails do not communicate inflection, tone, or mood. Red Hot had a date scheduled with MooMan. On his way to meet up with her, MooMan texted, "Hey, what do you want to do tonight?"

Red Hot texted back, "Whatever."

MooMan turned his car around and drove back to Moo-rristown. Red Hot was simply being easy-going and agreeable, but MooMan took the text in a negative way. He was probably letting disappointment from his past determine his attitude.

Red Hot said, "He's too MOOdy." She dumped him.

INTRAPERSONAL LEARNERS: You have superb self-understanding and appear calm, self-assured, and self-aware.

As a banker, every year I was forced to attend multiple, eight-hour classes on sales skills. One trainer was a severely Michigan accented, break-time smoking lady. She reminded my assistant manager Adele of the strong and feminine wrestler Chyna, so we called her that. We much preferred our comical, self-deprecating trainer Buttercuff, but Chyna specialized in certain products and procedures, so the bank Enterprised her in from Nashville.

She was teaching us how to coach subordinates and asked us "Why is it better to use open-ended questions when asking an employee to reflect on his or her efforts?"

I said, "Any time you can get an employee to articulate how he did well or how he messed up, he becomes more self-aware. When I was a teacher, I learned that self-awareness is the highest form of intelligence."

Not five minutes later, Chyna said something like, "Guys, some of these concepts are difficult for our coworkers, but, you see, I'm very self-aware, so I understand."

No joke, reader, she worked in "I am very self-aware" at least seven times before the lunch break.

People who are self-aware don't say they are self-aware. Confident intrapersonal learners welcome solitude. They define their own self-worth. Red Hot, who is such a learner, says to online browsers, "Don't like me? Fine. Click *next* to see more results." Red Hot offers these tips for those of you who are wooing an intrapersonal learner:

- o Don't be a smart mouth and call out someone for something she says on the profile page. Verbal abuse is not the ideal way to start a relationship.
- o Intrapersonal learners are the hardest fish to catch because they know precisely what they need and are self-sufficient. Don't offer to be a hero. It's insulting.
- o Do offer to be an equal partner.
- o Single parents, especially, don't want to carry you financially, emotionally, or otherwise.
- o Chauvinists and male-bashers need not apply.
- o Don't reach out to someone if you know you will never go out with her. These learners know when they are being played, and they might report you to the dating forum moderator.
- o Do remember to search and comment with caution. There's no back button in online dating.

Red Hot's profile reads, "Make my life better or don't bother."

VERBAL/LINGUISTIC LEARNERS: You learn best through language. You influence others through written and spoken language.

Don't trash the queen's English unless you seek a lover who "don't know how to talk proper." There, not *their*, not *they're,* are many ways to turn off a potential love interest. Spell check and proofread to find the kind of lovin' you need.

Do be academically realistic. She can't be Jenny to your Forrest.

Don't be silly. Pen, "I'll tell you later," and Red Hot will click the little x box now.

Grownups, it is rude to be shy. It is rude to be coy. Nobody has time for that juvenile nonsense.

If you end a courtship, tell him/her why. Don't leave an online dater hanging in cyberspace to wonder through an infinite number of reasons why he/she was dumped by a stranger.

Do be honest. If you really want to meet someone, take the time to write a respectful, detailed, and well-thought-out profile. Don't copy and paste. If you plagiarize online, you'll cheat in real life.

DON'T choose a username that refers to any body part, tapping something, or references minors. Red Hot listed usernames she has seen. She and I wrote responses to each. Be specific. I detest when, in a group setting, the leader says, "Introduce yourself and tell the group something interesting we may not know about you." Without fail, some dud says, "I can't think of anything interesting." Does that mean you can't think? Or that you are completely dull? Those are my conclusions. If nothing else, say, "I am very self-aware" and watch what happens. Learn from this.

Usernames	Our Responses
HotSnake	Get some Desitin
NeedsDate	You're advertising that you're advertising?
WalterBHot	So B we, but who B hotter?
SweetManWV	Says your last sister-cousin-lover.
TapperDude	Snare or bass?
RockEnd	Which end?
HotBeachLover	You love hot beaches? Watch those misplaced modifiers.
UsedEasyGoer	Herpes?
Kabobbin	For ka-apples?
VocalMan	You sound bossy.
HotMel	As in diner?
TheEasy	What?
TNTeachingStud	OMG we work together.
WildWhat'sHisName	Looking to settle down?
AloneNow[Name]	What will I have to fix?
FlyDrive	This is a no-fly zone.
Twerkin	Not at your age.
LongPutter	Four!

Do the best you can. I wish you luck, and I hope you'll increase your odds by Red Hot's hard-earned information and some make-up.

If you do find true love online and have a romantic rendezvous, don't get all flustered and forget something important. I found this jewel when beachcombing on Orange Beach during spring break a few years ago. Am I lucky or what?

Seashells and shattered dreams

Theory 24: There is no such thing as natural beauty.

Just after I rough drafted this concept, I went for my first mammogram to make sure Atlantic and Pacific were healthy. You know, people over 40 go on all sorts of medical adventures. Yippee!

I'm not going to lie. I was nervous. I am not immune to tragedy. I panic about certain things because those things have happened to me or to someone close to me. I'm no better/different/more important than my dear friends who are breast cancer survivors. Tall Child's best friend, Character with Character, said, as he lay dying from colon cancer, "I am sick of those pink ribbons all over the place. Where's the stuff about colon and stomach cancer?"

I told him, "The Komen people are better at marketing." My dear friend Baton Swiper works year-round to fundraise through the local Komen office out of respect for her beloved late mother-in-law. I don't enter the mammogram room with superficial naiveté.

Good Friday 2014, I handed over my insurance card and turned to find a seat among other pensive patients. I saw a glimmer of hope in a framed, signed photo of none other than my hero Dolly. The queen of boobies, creativity, and positive energy was there. I felt better, calmer, until 30 minutes later when the x-ray technician squeezed Pacific for just a smidge longer than she had squeezed Atlantic and explained, "I just want to make sure I got a *really good* picture." Gulp. Then came the wave of anxiety. I cried all the way to my car.

I knew it, I thought. You see, people who suffer anxiety disorder always "know it." We waste hours, if not days, of our lives worrying about things that may never happen. We can't control it. Exercise, strong talks from Southern mamas, church, and wine help. Oh, and medicine. Medicine is the best help of all. Sometimes my sweet friend Agape Agave gets quiet or confused. When asked if she's okay, she drops her voice and moans like Eor, "It's my meeediccinnne."

I chastised myself, *Why did I go on a Friday? Ugh! Now I have a weekend of worrying.* The following Monday, a nurse called and asked me to come back, just like I knew she would. The MOMENT I walked back into the lobby I ran smack into my young teaching colleague who was fighting breast cancer. The first thing I thought when I saw her was, *Beautiful*. She wore a head covering, so all I could see was her face. Her beautiful face. Her cherubic smile, formerly framed by blonde curls, was flawless. We enjoyed a quick academic discussion about school and about her treatments. Her beautiful mind. She cheered me on when I explained I'd been called back in for a second look. *She* cheered *me* on. Her beautiful soul.

The routine mammogram machine is like a plastic Panini maker; it's a gentle squeeze for someone my size, but not too grilling. The "call-back" appointment is a bit involved, with two distinct procedures. The first is like a George Foreman Grill: it optimizes health, squeezes out the fat, and focuses on one big chunk of meat. Think slow hammer to red clay. The second procedure is like a pasta-maker. Think grinder to dough ball. I had to lean over and drop Pacific down between two plastic boxes. The x-ray technician got under me and tucked and pulled Pacific into place. I said, "I wonder whose view is better. Yours or mine." The boxes pressed together and turned the dough ball (which is big enough to make chicken and dumplings for a tent revival) into a No-Yolk egg noodle. Ouch!

After the squeezes. I visited the "Complementary Boutique," a gift shop that sells all things girly and breast cancer patient. I hoped to find an industrial-strength Miracle Suit. The clerk asked me how she could help me, and I said, "I know this sounds shallow, but do you have a fake C breast I can see and feel? I'm dreaming of having breast reduction surgery and would like to see how I could end up looking. Plus, I just had my first mammogram, and I'm nervous about the results. Those pink ribbons are everywhere." She had no fake breasts lying around. She had something better. Peace of mind. She said, "I used to look in the mirror and see everything that was wrong with me. Now I look in the mirror and say to myself, 'Look how strong you are!'" She's a cancer survivor. That's what my friend Flower Child calls a God wink—when God answers in a quick, poignant sign. Results came. Long 34J-long-story-short, I was okay.

I texted Red Hot Backspace that my doctors found a cluster of cysts near the Jersey Shore and one rogue cyst floating solo in the South Pacific. "Bali Hai!" Let's now explore how we may become beautiful.

Physical Beauty

As a child, I didn't have all the clothes I *thought* I needed. I wore flannel shirts and thick Lee jeans from a Goody's store in Sevierville because that's what my parents could afford. Everyone else wore slick jumpsuits with matching Reebok high-tops and twist-a-bead necklaces. In my sophomore yearbook picture, I'm wearing a *Les Miserable* T-shirt tucked into pants a junior handed down to me. My clothes have always been sub-par. Tall Child calls me a "fashion disaster."

During our personal recession—brought on by an avalanche of issues (tornado, infertility treatments, the lost battle between Sharky's permanent teeth and the school gym floor, my adult education, and adopting Gnome), my wardrobe and our home took a beating. I have some beautiful friends with beautiful homes in The 9-1-9. All of their plumbing works all of the time. If something breaks, they call a repairman, write the check, and suffer minor inconvenience. At our house, when something breaks, I freak out. Tall Child hides. From me. Sometime during our personal recession, we went to a dress-up party at one of those gorgeous, fully-functioning homes. I wore some tired, God-awful outfit and came back to my old 1956 house, feeling down. A day or so later, I stumbled across one of my now favorite Bible verses:

Consider the lilies how they grow: they toil not, they spin not; and yet I say unto you, that Solomon in all his glory was not arrayed like one of these. Luke 12:27 (KJV)

I chewed on that verse for days. It liberated me. I needed that verse in high school. So many boys and girls need that verse in high school.

Here's a little perspective for you on the importance of clothing. My friend P is a retired gym teacher. She lives in Downtown Knoxville. She buys her shorts at thrift shops because they are "softer" when you buy them there. She spends her time and energy on people, not things. She traveled to Africa with her son. She told me, "There I was on a safari in the middle of the Kenyan plains, and one of those Maasai nomad guys came out of nowhere to sell us hand-carved wooden animals. He wore a sheet-skirt, sandals, beads around his neck, piercings, and a Tennessee Lady Vols basketball T-shirt from the '80s! How many people do you think have worn that old shirt?"

Mini-Theory: What comes out of your home matters way more than what goes into it.

Behavioral Beauty

As my grandmama Buddy used to say, "Pretty is as pretty does." Red Hot Backspace co-wrote the previous chapter because she felt a kind need to help singletons navigate cyberspace romance. A few days ago, she said, "Dating at my age ain't easy." She referenced scars, both physical and emotional, that must be explained. But I see her in a different light. I see her as someone who has learned great lessons, triumphed over tragedy, and earned three college degrees. Her sense of humor was the light in my school days and she is SMART. What a prize package!

When the rare boy asked me out, and I told Delicious he wasn't cute, she'd say, "If you start liking him, he'll get cuter." Well, the opposite is also true.

Teachers will relate to this concept, for sure. Have you ever met someone you thought was attractive, but as his behavior got ugly, he got less physically attractive?

One of the students I tutor wrote his college application essay, titled "Happiness in the shape of a chicken nugget," to illustrate lessons he learned while working at Chick-Fil-A. He compared a ten-year-old Liberian refugee and a privileged Chick-Fil-A customer. In his youthful, yet insightful interpretation, he noted that the boy who had nothing was inherently happier than the woman who "had everything." The Liberian boy was appreciative. The woman was rude. My student told me, "She was dressed up in expensive clothes with her hair all fixed and lots of makeup on."

I asked, "Pretty?"

He answered, "Ugly."

Spiritual Beauty

Tell yourself you are pretty! Delicious has always battled her weight, but she's also extremely confident. I pondered this unique aspect of her personality and asked her for clarification. She explained, "Bug, I think that when you have a pretty face, you don't really notice how fat you are. Look at all those runners on the side of the road. They are skinny, but they look miserable, and they all need lipstick. Delta Burke is beautiful, and she is almost as fat as I am."

I don't have a belly button. Instead, I have a hideous scar where tubes fed me and kept me alive in the newborn intensive care unit at Columbus, Georgia, Medical Center in 1974. I have an uglier scar on my right thigh where I guess the tubes came out. I have cellulite, prickly chin hairs that regenerate like starfish, which is why I can never hike the Appalachian Trail or be imprisoned, and my forefingers are twisted funny. Who cares?

Having said this, I firmly believe that women should do the best they can with what they have, be proud of their femininity, and wear makeup. Whether I wake up on a houseboat on Norris Lake, in a tent in the Smoky Mountains, or in an overcrowded beach house with five mamas and fifteen children, I slap on my Cover Girl. Why? Because I want to feel good about myself and because I look like bleached dog dumplings without it. I am not naturally beautiful. I don't do Botox or facials. I cannot tan. I get my haircut at Great Clips. I buy my cosmetics at the grocery store because I'm frugal and I get asthma attacks from mall makeup departments. So, between frozen pizzas and cat litter, I select blush, eyeshadow, normal to dry foundation, and assorted other necessities so that no one has to see me bare-faced. "Knoxville! This is for you!"

Beauty grows from tragedy, experience, and education. Life may wear our bodies down, but it makes us spiritually beautiful and of much more service to one another. Why not cap off all that hard-earned loveliness with some Revlon Red lipstick? Confidence is a beautiful trait.

I asked Tall Child, "Do you think there is such a thing as natural beauty?"

"Sure," he said. "Everybody has something."

"What do you mean?" I asked. "Elaborate."

He said, "Well, everybody has something beautiful on his body or about his personality. Like my legs."

When Sharky was a gangly pre-teen, he was mouthy. In the car one day, I asked, "What is wrong with you the last few days? Why are you being such a smarty pants?"

He sighed, "I think my pheromones are coming in."

Say what?

I found the definition for pheromones on athenainstitute.com. The Greeks knew everything. The site reads, "Pheromones are naturally occurring odorless substances the fertile body excretes externally, conveying an airborne signal that provides information to, and triggers responses from, the opposite sex of the same species."

Well, now I understand why no one asked me out in high school. I am infertile, so I didn't excrete any signals to the boys. Yes, I birthed Sharky, but my fertility doctor said there is no medical explanation for him. After six miserable years of fertility treatments and two years in the domestic adoption process, we met Gnome's birthmother Tinkerbell and adopted baby Gnome. Now, that's a great story, and it's in another book titled *The Eye of Adoption*.

Okay, back to natural beauty. Since Sharky was so in tune with "pretty is as pretty does," I decided to interview him for this Theory.

Bug: *When I say, "There is no such thing as natural beauty, what does that mean to you?"*
Sharky: *You can't just grow up to be beautiful. You have to* transform.
Bug: *What else?*
Sharky: *That's all I know.*
Bug: *What else? What do you mean* transform*?*
Sharky: *You must process through it.*
Bug: *Through what?*
Sharky: *Stages.*
Bug: *Stages of what?*
Sharky: *Stuff. Physical. Mental.*
Bug: *When you say process through stages, what do you mean?*
Sharky: *You must process through them to become a real person.*
Bug: *Nobody's going to hear this but me. (Um . . .) Do you mean a child is not a real person?*

Sharky: *No, you process to become an adult and have a good life.*
Bug: *In my book, I'm writing about physical, behavioral, and spiritual beauty. What do you have to do to become physically beautiful?*
Sharky: *Moisturize.*
Bug: *What do you have to do to become* behaviorally *beautiful?*
Sharky: *You think on the bright side. You* decide *you are pretty.*
Bug: *What about spiritually beautiful?*
Sharky: *Ask God if you are pretty.*

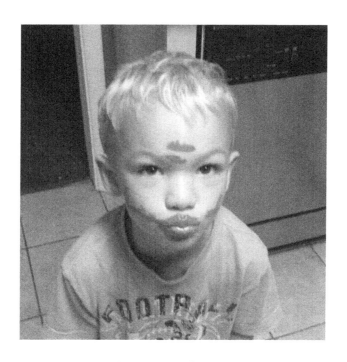

Pretty Baby Gnome found my stash.

Theory 25: Chunky girls need love songs too, especially in the summertime.

Summer should be carefree, but, since there's no such thing as natural beauty, summer also brings an embarrassing, hard to avoid circumstance that causes us great anxiety and self-hatred.

We must wear underwear in public.

Delicious once stated, quite profoundly, that she looks better *naked* than she does in a swimsuit. I don't know about naked, but I do look better in my underwear than I do in a swimsuit. Why? Because my bras are designed with suspension engineering, volume control, orthopedic support, and coverage. In a swimsuit, I feel loose, droopy, and exposed.

I lose and gain the SAME few pounds every stinking week. The schedule typically works like this:

Monday: I get motivated and go "low-carb" and drop the pounds by Thursday.

Thursday: My britches don't put a red gash in my backfat. I get cocky. I eat some bread.

Friday/Saturday/Sunday: Agape Agave, Flower Child, Smokin' Scrubs, Pearl, and Elaine text up a trip to El Charro, or I sit in the river with a tall insulated cup of pure freakin' joy. Note: Pearl was formerly nicknamed Downton Gams, but she has evolved. Also, she wears pearls to work, on hikes, at vacation Bible school, in the grocery store, and probably even when she soaks in her Dr. Teal's Epsom salt baths. Classic.

Monday: I beat myself up and start all over. Then I go to Zumba and try not to laugh at myself in the gigantic mirrors.

I think it's so ironic that when I'm dressed in a tight-fitting, rib-gouging underwire tankini, sitting scrunched over in a bag chair, and sweating like a chubby piccolo player at band camp in August, I get hungry. What is that all about? Nothing about that scene is appetizing, but of course I can't see me. The plastic Adirondack chairs are much more flattering because you lean back a little. The bag chairs are like canvas fat sacks with lily white legs dangling out the front. At least they have cup holders.

One evening, Tall Child declared, "For the first time in my life, I have a gut hanging over my belt." Poor guy.

He asked me to help him lose weight. I said, "First, you have to eat breakfast to wake up your metabolism."

He argued, "I don't eat breakfast. I can skip that."

I argued back, "You have to eat breakfast."

He said, "How do you know that?"

I said, "Never question a 45-year-old woman about dieting. No matter how fat we *are*, we all know precisely *how* to lose weight."

Yep, we *know*. Why can't we follow through? It could be that…

- Society and our husbands want us thin, so we rebel.
- We love ourselves and like to treat ourselves to wine, onion dip, and ice cream with peanut butter mixed in.
- Eating too much is a secondary concern compared to the daily issues we face: working, raising children, staying married, needy friends, menopause, PMS, pregnancy, infertility, committees, addictions, caring for aging parents, going back to school, expensive car/house/health problems.
- Bad news throws us off. For example, I was doing great on my diet and not planning to drink Pinot Grigio one day. Then, TWO dentists called within one hour of each other and told me how much Gnome's gomper crowns (gym rat=candy consumption so Mama can watch Sharky play=cavities) and Sharky's braces would cost. I went straight to the FAFSA site but apparently you can't get student loans unless someone is in college. Whatever. That evening I went to Food City to get Tall Child and me some low carb salad ingredients for supper. The stress-induced magnetic pull toward the wine cooler was overwhelming. I blame the dentists. Bad news brings about bad food.
- We watch so many zombie shows that we eat as much as we can now because we subconsciously believe one day we we'll be stabbing our undead neighbors in their foreheads to gain access to their dusty apocalyptic pantries.
- We women do ALL the cooking. Tall Child will announce via text or phone mid-day, "I am going to eat one can of

extra spicy, no-bean chili for supper." There are four people in this house. FOUR.

- Taking mood medicine and hormone therapy jacks up metabolism, but not taking mood medicine and hormone therapy jacks up peace in the household.
- We face tremendous peer pressure at work. When my best friend Pearl returned to the teaching profession, she packed on a few pounds. She expressed self-hatred for her weight gain. I advised, "Pearl, when you work all week, you gain weight. I think the problem is that stress hormone Cortisol." She said, "I think the problem is that there's a cake in the teachers' lounge every single day."

What can we do? If we read magazines, we feel worse. Articles tell us to drink eight full glasses of water every day. That's a full glass every two hours. Water has no taste, so I what is the incentive? Plus, some people, particularly educators, are trapped. Even if they can drink all day, they have few bathroom breaks. You can't leave thirty middle-schoolers unattended. Ask any family practice doctor; he/she will tell you that teachers have two consistent problems— TMJ from clenching their teeth trying not to curse and bladder infections. Articles tell us to sleep eight hours. Um, on what planet is that possible? I sleep like a fat beagle on mamaw's back porch: one eye open, ready to chase a rabid raccoon away from my babies. Plus, Gnome doesn't sleep. I keep hoping he's one of those geniuses who simply doesn't need rest, but I think he just likes to party. Articles advise us to exercise. We should park on the outskirts of the parking lot, take the stairs, do pushups from our desks, butt clenches on the commute. Magazines teach us to eat super healthy foods like avocado with shrimp and salmon with brussels sprouts. Want your coworkers to hate you? Reheat salmon and brussels sprouts in the breakroom.

Maybe one day I'll do a test and try all of the above and report back. Until then, I'm throwing in the beach towel and embracing my pounds. I think I'll even name them. Hmmm. What would be most appropriate for a few pudgy friends that show up every weekend?

Perhaps I should name them after their lineage.

Pound 1: Mayfield (as in onion dip and ice cream)
Pound 2: Bota (as in Box)
Pound 3: Jose (as in my favorite waiter at El Charro)
Pound 4: Mailbox (as in all the stress from snail mail bills that incite
     me to gobble and guzzle)
Pound 5: Liberty (as in I hate authority, so stop telling me to drink
     water, exercise, and eat salmon)

By the way, I need to lose more than five pounds. Mayfield, Bota, Jose, Mailbox, and Liberty have plenty of company.

Who can (or should) resist the ice cream truck?

To encourage all of you less-than-svelte ladies who must wear underwear in public this summer, and worse, like me, must wear underwear in public while chasing a roaming Gnome, I rewrote a song. I chose Luke Bryan's, "Country Girl Shake it for Me." I strongly suggest you listen to the real song a couple of times before you read/sing my lyrics. That way you'll know the tune. Shows are always better when you know the music in advance. I'm no thespian, but I do love Broadway musicals, especially when they come to my town and I don't have to navigate subways and airports and get dressed in steaming hotel bathrooms. Is it me, or does everyone's skin look haggard in those mirrors? My aunt Big Booty J (BBJ) agrees. During a stay at the Columbus, Georgia, Hampton Inn, she said to Delicious and me, "You really don't realize how fat you are until you stay in a motel." As a frequent visitor to all traveling shows who come within a nine-mile radius of my house *when* I have enough writin' money to go see somethin', I assure that you'll enjoy *Les Miserables* if you translate the title and buy the CD first. Here's my parody of Luke's song. I can call him by his first name because Agape Agave, a massage therapist, got to work on him during his show at Thompson-Boling Arena in Knoxville. I hug her, she rubs him, we are friends. Right, right, Agape?

"*Chunky* Girl Shake it for Me" – satirized (which covers my copyright a$$) by Bug and dedicated to every self-conscious woman ever

Hey girl. Go on now.
You know you've got everybody looking.

Got a little donk in your big white truck,
Take off your swim skirt; don't cover that up!
Stomp your size nine boots in the Georgia mud,
Dip that chip; make me fall in love,

Get up on the hood of my tractor, that's hot!
Be careful, don't trip, you'll need a tetanus shot.
We can't drive to the after-hours clinic with a buzz,
You'd lose your teaching license.
We'd have to put the pimento cheese up.
Let's play it safe, stay here, and eat boiled peanuts.

Straddle that hood with your thunder thighs.
I'll turn on "Dixieland Delight."
Get all parts moving, I can't wait,
To watch you do your thing!

Shake it for the young girls dreading bikini season,
For the sexy mamaws out there canning and freezing,
For the Weight Watchers, Low Carb-ers, and gluten-dodgers,
We know they ain't having fun.

Shake it for the Cross-Fitters who never enjoy a cone,
For the pageant girls marching to their mothers' drones,
For the teenagers building their self-esteem.
For the fat band geeks. They're living the dream!

Chunky girl, shake it for me girl,
Shake it for me girl, shake it for me
Chunky girl, shake it for me girl,
Shake it for me girl, shake it for me.

Somebody's pudgy little pretty child,
Met a Little Debbie, got double-wide.
You know how to *live*, you know how to fry.
Rope me in with your custard pie.

So come on over here and crank this arm,
Spin me and this rock salt with your buttery charm.
You could be the woman of my dreams,
Let's make some chunky loving and homemade ice cream.
Yeah, yeah, yeah!

Shake it for the young girls dreading bikini season,
For the sexy mamaws out there canning and freezing,
For the Weight Watchers, Low Carb-ers, and gluten-dodgers,
We know they ain't having fun.

Shake it for the Cross-Fitters who never enjoy a cone,
For the pageant girls marching to their mothers' drones,
For the teenagers building their self-esteem.
For the fat band geeks. They're living the dream!

Chunky girl, shake it for me girl,
Shake it for me girl, shake it for me.

It is OKAY to be pale in July. I lather on the Jergens Fair to Medium self-tanner, but it's a waste of time because it doesn't cover my spider veins.

Reader, for the love of summer, have <u>fun</u>. Don't be unhealthy, but please drop the self-doubt, self-hatred, and self-sabotaging baggage. Start your diets in the fall (or never), and LIVE! Have the same attitude toward yourself that your friends who love you have toward you! And remember, when you flop into that suspect tube to ride the rapids, hold on to your Yeti/Arctic/store brand tumbler and enjoy the ride.

Bug, Smokin' Scrubs, and Flower Child have healthy attitudes toward fun *and* know what to do with rope and a cinderblock.

Theory 26: 40+ is the perfect age.

My 40th birthday party cake, designed by OMGG

My friends and family enjoyed harassing me through the turn to 40 on February 14, 2014. Bop sent me a series of funny cards; each enclosed a $5 bill. Is there such a thing as a $500 bill? If so, that would have been better. Dogwood Deb, and my nieces Balloon Girl and Cake had a pink and red flower arrangement delivered to my junior high classroom. Reader, if you think teenagers want to "fit in" you'd be amazed at how teachers do their best to draw no special attention. Why? Because they don't want to have the same conversation 75 times in one day. I'm bold.

"Is it your birthday, Mrs. Bug?"
"Yes."
"How old are you?"
"I'm 40."
 "Dang girl, you're looking good."
"I thought you were a lot older."
"You're older than my mom."
"Mrs. Bug, how old is your husband?"
"He's 51."

"That's like me dating my geometry teacher. Gross!
"What time does he go to bed?"

The balloon and flower delivery, combined with a school day shortened three hours for a minor snowpocalypse, made for an eventful third period with 35 freshmen.

Look, I love attention like Gnome loves candy. I enjoy public speaking and being the center of attention. But, I'm not big on birthdays. I suck at them. I forget to buy birthday cards. I forget to call people. I kind of forget to even care. That sounds awful, doesn't it? Sorry. Selfish? Sorry again. I don't discriminate, however. I don't care about my birthday, either. Those of us with anxiety disorders likely associate birthdays with milestones, the passage of time that can never be recovered or relived, and, truthfully, <u>death</u>. On February 14 each year, I thank God I'm alive and get through the day. Yes, it is Valentine's Day. I'm lucky for that because most people are distracted. For example, every February 14 around supper time, I hand Tall Child a "For Husband" Valentine and he says, "Oh, Bug! Let's trade cards later." We eat supper. Then, Tall Child says, "I have to take care of something really quickly. I'll be right back." He makes a mad dash to Walgreens and comes home with a proud grin and two cards: a "For Wife" Valentine card and a "For Her" birthday card. Every year. Bless his Tall, kind, forgetful heart.

I think Tall Child has finally caught my fever of apathy. On his 50th birthday, our friends wanted to throw him a toga party as a nod to his youthful adventures and baby-booming swagger, but he declined, "Let's just let this one *sliiide on by*."

Maybe I have some disregard for my birthday *because* it's on Valentine's Day, and, except for Tall Child and my college sweetheart, Nixon Lover, who was, ironically, also born on Valentine's Day 1974, I never had a boyfriend on February 14. The sting of an empty locker and no call from the office to pick up a vase of roses never leaves. Why, male GPHS Highlanders? Why? Was it my sharp tongue, hallway scowls, the fact that you had to pass Delicious's twelfth grade English class to graduate, or my lack of pheromones? Maybe my proclamation of virginity til marriage got in the way. I should have sent myself flowers. I've learned so much since high school. I buy myself cases of wine nowadays just for getting a paycheck. What's the difference?

This is a good time to more formally introduce The Owl Squad. Thanks to The Owl Squad's acceptance of me through every mistake, embarrassing moment, added pound, and passing year, I've learned from them how to accept myself. And, at 40, I am free. As Delicious once said, "You girls know how to let the rough side drag."

Pearl has signature style. Her classy, yet casual look consists of long-sleeved shirts, corduroys, preppy-yet-colorful loafers, and fitted down vests topped off with pearls, honey. Pearls. Pearl is a mix of British composure, European style, Land's End practicality, and Old Southern tradition. And, in summertime, men of The 9-1-9 are treated to Cherokee tanned, smooth kneed perfection strutting out of her Patagonia hiking skorts. She's a passionate mother and a fantastic sounding board for a loon like me. I confessed to her, "I'm afraid folks are going to make a big deal about my birthday."

She said, "Don't you worry about that, Bug, just get through it. I was so glad to see that number come and go. No big deal. No big deal. That's that. Done. Done. Forty. Done."

Agape Agave is "Agape" because she loves circles around you! Her instinct is unconditional, country-style, custard pie love. She's "Agave" because she makes a mean beverage with a plant product of the same name. Agape Agave can quilt, sew, and can tomatoes. She refers to herself as "Mamaw." She is master of the pressure cooker and owns four ducks. I asked her, "What do you think is good about turning 40?"

Agape Agave said, "Let me tell you what my mama said. She said to me, 'Oh, honey, just wait til you're 40. You won't give a damn what anybody says to you.'" Mamaw Agape Agave's mama was right.

If I want to dance, I dance, thanks to inspiration from my smart, physically-fit friend Elaine. Elaine loves the stage. She belongs on the stage. When Elaine takes the dance floor, she elevates the entire party to a new level of interest and excitement. She's a fantastic live auction item floor model. She's excels at stretching.

Elaine performs best when joined on stage by Smokin' Scrubs, our gorgeous blonde member who is a natural born tambourine player. She laughs and loves wide open. And, she sleeps in her deceased father's medical scrubs. She misses him. A nurse by trade, she emits a soulful, healing laugh. As soon as she spots a tambourine, she hops on stage to play and sing. I've never really heard her sing. Can she? Regardless, she's so good-looking a band of doctors called Second Opinion hired her to sing backup.

What we Owls lack in talent, we make up with stage presence.

Flower Child also inspires me to relax. Flower Child is a 9-1-9 neighborhood leader in compassion, philanthropy, and kindness. A vacation Bible school veteran, she exudes peace. She is the queen of tolerance and acceptance. Her mantra? "I love people." She also loves tie-dye and comfort. Back when I was a blazer-bound banker, I told Flower Child I was sick of figuring out what would fit and what to wear every morning. I said, "Even shoes. I am sick of going through my pathetic closet of tight pants and dusty shoes. I need a uniform."

Flower Child said, "I wear only two pairs of shoes ever. Flip-flops if it's warm. Uggs if it's cold."

It's true. We went to a fancy party at country club when the roads were ICED over, and my house could not rise above 50 degrees. Flower Child wore a flowing, navy blue, floor length gown. And Uggs. I still have SUV PTSD from our slide down my driveway.

So free. So, so free.

I'm writing, obviously, from my own perspective and experience, but I think many of you 40-and-overs will relate. The rest of you can anticipate landing on this happy number. What do I mean? Why is 40+ the perfect age?

At 40+, I judge less and don't care if I'm judged. Delicious and Pooh taught me well, but much of my newfound confidence and free thinking comes from two experiences. First, adopting Gnome in 2010 and continuing an open adoption with his birth family widened my perspective on love, human nature, and parenting. The eight-year journey from infertility to meeting Gnome for the first time was embedded with enlightenment beyond anything I ever expected. Second, I stopped seeking approval from others. While growing up, like many of you, I felt misunderstood. I still do, but I don't care! I steer clear of people who might use me or abuse me. As Pooh used to say, "I always like the people who like me."

I don't give a flip when people criticize me. I wrote my book, *The Eye of Adoption*, to help other women affected by infertility and adoption. Imagine wanting to become pregnant but your body and medical experts telling you it's impossible. Imagine the depth of that loss and frustration. *The Eye of Adoption* has ministered to thousands of women. Through it, I've made friends all over the world. But, when you write a book, or make any creative work public, even when its purpose is pure and positive, you subject yourself to bad reviews, critical commentary, and ridicule. Ridicule is especially hurtful when it comes from family. The day my book went live on Amazon, word got around. Immediately, my book's cover image and friendly messages of congratulations exploded across my social media footprint. Amazon and Kindle order numbers grew and validated my work. That Friday, I attended a birthday party for a little cousin. No one at that party mentioned my book. No one. And, it was obvious, as it always is to women, that some of the people there had been talking about me before I arrived. My stomach turned. I did not understand until later that a few things I wrote upset them. Then an ugly "review" showed up on Amazon.com. It's still there. It hurt and haunted me for days until one of my ninth grade students read it aloud in my technology class. Those freshmen had known me all year long. I had talked at length about the book's content and goals. When the boy read it aloud, the entire class erupted in a mix of laughter (at the reviewer) and outrage. Their perspectives put that critical "review" in perspective for me. I should thank the person who gave me one star. She guided me over a big hump. Now, I write freely and concentrate on audiences who can appreciate my efforts.

I'm not in bondage to name brands or nice cars or fancy clothes. I grew up in an old farmhouse and, for some crazy reason, bought another old house. At 26 years old, I wore myself out trying to make my 1956 plumbing nightmare of a house pretty and perfect with the right touches. Keeping up an old house while raising two children and working full time while married to a Tall Child is, well, a losing battle. The oddities no longer make me drive to Home Depot. They make me laugh.

Gnome splashes in his orange tub under peach and cream tiles.

I desperately needed a laptop, mostly for mobility to dodge Gnome, Sharky, and Tall Child when I write. One year I begged my immediate and extended family to all chip in together. "Skip clothes, earrings, stationery, and junk. Whatever you would normally spend on me, pile it together and buy me a simple laptop." For a YEAR, I hinted and outright begged for this basic tool. Christmas came. I got athletic socks from Dick's. A week after Christmas, I spotted a friend's twelve-year-old daughter. I asked, "What did Santa Claus bring you?"

"A laptop," she said.

Ah, The 9-1-9.

I don't beat myself up about what I eat or how I look. Well, I am a girl. Let's just say I don't obsess, and I'm quite forgiving. I wear make-up because there's no such thing as natural beauty, and if I don't wear it, people wouldn't recognize me. Because I'm a pale, Appalachian girl, make-up *gives* me a face. Imagine blue dots on a Chinet platter. Once, in college, I made a post-shower, Maybelline-free, late-night run to the dorm lobby for a Twix. I spotted my then boyfriend's best friend. We made eye contact. I said, "Hey." He said it back. Later that week, I teased him, "What were you doing in Humes Hall so late the other night?"

He said, "How did you know I was in Humes Hall?"

I don't worry about finding the right clothes like I did in my twenties and early thirties. I'm contemplating a company uniform. What do you think an East Tennessee writer should wear? I need to look intelligent, responsible, and eccentric. Diane Keaton wears white. Whoopi Goldberg covers her entire body in a weird turtleneck-burqa-toga-sweatshirt combo. I'm leaning toward Simon Cowell's style of T-shirt and jeans, but my stomach is too fat for my jeans right now, and Delicious says I'm too old to wear denim. I'm thinking sports bra, shift, and flip flops.

I don't seek perfection—from myself or from others. An acquaintance admitted to me, "Once someone does me wrong, I cut him or her out of my life." She's going to run out of people. Every time someone "does me wrong" or hurts my feelings, I repeat two mantras of forgiveness: "Seventy times seven" and "Put not your faith in man." These are my abbreviated versions of Matthew 18:22 and Psalm 146.

It's raining laundry!

63

As a student, I competed against others and myself for higher grades and recognition. As a young wife, mother, and bank manager, I was frantic and ambitious, a real "Type A." Now, I strive for A's in people and career and am satisfied with passing grades in housework. My goal is not to avoid mistakes, as they are inevitable. My goal is to make progress from them. Delicious preaches, "Always anticipate the incompetence of others." Well, there's no limit to what I can't do!

I'm terribly flawed, yet seeking self-awareness, mostly for the sake of others. I've watched myself for a while now and noted a few things that bother me (and likely bother others). I'm loud in classrooms and restaurants and houses. I throw temper tantrums and toss Tupperware. I'm destructive. Delicious says I always rushed and "screwed up one side of the poster board" when I did science projects, and she always had to drive back to the store for another poster board. I always wondered why, if she knew me so well, she didn't buy two poster boards in the first place. She recently explained that she couldn't afford two. Shame on me. Anyway, throughout my life I denied these flaws. Now, I embrace them, write about them, and try really hard to control the impulse to sling a light bulb at Tall Child.

I understand that I can't control other adult people. I won't even try, well, until after I'm dead. If Tall Child won't get a checkup, shame on him. Other than Sharky and Gnome and myself, I am not responsible for another person's healthcare decisions. Tall Child, Delicious, and I hired an attorney to write up our wills. In our meeting, I said, "I want to make sure that Tall Child's next wife doesn't take anything from Sharky and Gnome. Draw that up."

Tall Child announced to the room, "I am not getting married ever again."

Then we discussed the living wills, a.k.a., the pulling of plugs. Delicious said, "Keep me alive at all costs for as long as possible."

Tall Child and I completed the Do Not Resuscitate forms. Tall Child said, "Who will pull my plug?"

Delicious said, "I will."

Delicious doesn't like my choice, but I now know that I am not responsible for another person's reaction to one of my decisions. Chronic worriers, guilt trippers, pushy friends, manipulators, and whiny children no longer affect me. Delicious is ahead of me on this issue. All of the ladies in her Sunday school class wanted to go to lunch after "big church." Delicious said, "I think I'll just go home."

They begged, "Oh, come on. We will have fun. We will even let you pick the place. Please go!"

Delicious insisted, "I don't think I can."

"Why not?" they asked. "We'll even pay for your lunch. Why won't you go?" This went on for several minutes.

Tired and out of excuses, Delicious stated, "I just flat out don't want to go." She later told me, "I sounded like a mean Yankee and now I feel bad."

People in the South are masterful excuse-makers. We often tell way too much detail and do our best to not hurt other people's feelings, but sometimes people just don't take the first "No." Sometimes, you have to be blunt. I think the Sunday school ladies were good with it. I bet they got it out of their systems with all kinds of theories during their Delicious-free lunch. "I bet she forgot to wear deodorant again and it's always hot at Olive Garden." "Maybe she's broke." "Maybe she wants to finish a page in her coloring book." "Do you think she left the stove on?" "Maybe she drinks at lunchtime. We are Baptists." "Surely she ain't got no date."

I'm less inhibited and more plain-spoken in my "old age." Even the book description of *The Eye of Adoption* on Amazon reads, "Dyer tells it like it is." I figure people are worn out trying to figure things out, so I just write like I speak, perhaps with flaws but certainly with honesty. Readers relate. I trust myself. I know why I write what I write, and I write from my soul. Simple, trite, spiritual, funny, dull, who knows? I'm flattered if anyone reads my work. I've been accused of saying "whatever comes to mind," but I hold in about 80 percent. Be warned. I have nonsense to share with the world.

I don't feel guilty for taking care of myself. Agape Agave said, "All I want to do is diddle around on Pinterest, drink tons of coffee, and have everyone leave me the [heck] alone." Amen, sister wife. Do it. Women, at 40+, I finally have the guts to say, "Hey, Tall Child and boys, I'm going out to look for a bra and it will take a looooong time. Suck it up. And, unless you want me to burn up our Verizon minutes in a pre-menopausal, big breasted rage, don't call me while I'm sweating in a Dillard's dressing room." No. More. Guilt. Why, just yesterday I went to the grocery store all by myself. It was awesome!

I *need* other people to make choices for me. I have terrible taste in clothing and accessories. I have complete trust in my friends and family who buy me treats to wear. As a matter of fact, they know and embrace this fact! Generous, thoughtful Pearl gave me a Kate Spade handbag for my birthday! WHAAAAAT! It's from New. York. City. And it's beautiful. My last handbag was from The Walmart at the Walker Springs Exit on I-40. I asked Pearl how to fix my hair for a cotillion dance, and she said, emphatically, "We are curly girls. We cannot go straight; it just makes us look tired."

Waves it is, Pearl! Friskey on water introduced me to Stitch Fix. I like it. When I signed up, I told the online computer stylist thingy the following requirements for all shipments:

1. I must wear a bra at all times.
2. I am pale and look even paler in pale clothing.
3. No waistlines, elastic or otherwise, will be purchased.
4. The cheaper the better.
5. I am always casual.
6. I accept the Bohemian look.
7. No heels.

I've embraced my appearance, and I have lots of new and reduced things to celebrate!

1. Bigger, then smaller, but still big, boobs! Back in 2013, I visited Dillard's bra shop. Well, I plopped one day's worth of teacher wages on the biggest cup size sold at Dillard's. Here's the kicker/bouncer: I need the next size up. Really? *Really?* How much onion dip have I eaten? I broke down in the dressing room. At the time, I weighed about 155 pounds. I wish that were the case now. Anyway, in that sweaty, stressful, disgusting, marshmallowy moment, I decided to seek plastic surgery. BREAST REDUCTION. More on that (them) later.

UK 34
USA 34 H

1891 BLACK H 34 9760

340441 352335

$ 68.00

2. Old white woman booty. It's happening. My butt fat is rising up and out, just below my waist like a mushroom shelf over a giant coffee bean. The shelves will make great places for grandbabies to perch. It's all about perspective.

3. Bedazzled legs! I've gotten into constellations lately because Gnome is learning the lunar phases and stares up and gasps, "Look! Stars!" Well, I happen to sport similar wonders on my legs. So, if you are chipping in ideas for my "uniform," please stay away from colors that bring out the blue hues of my spider veins.

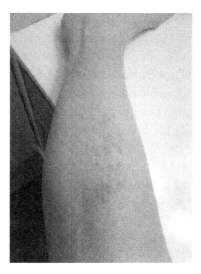

"I can see Halley's Comet!"

At 40, I happily share wisdom imparted to me by others. Tall Child (now age 56 with a healthy tummy per his low carb regimen) touts "50 is the new 40." I hope he's right. I've had a thing for proportional reasoning ever since my math instructional mentor "Certified Genius" taught me the following formula:

$$\frac{\textbf{Part}}{\textbf{Whole}} = \frac{\textbf{Part}}{\textbf{Whole}}$$

If 50 is the new 40, I am 36 years old and weigh 129.6.

$$\frac{50}{40} = \frac{45}{x} \qquad \frac{50}{40} \quad \frac{162}{x}$$

(40x45)/50=36   (40x162)/50=129.6

Dang, I'm young and SKINNY! Friend, master this concept, and you will increase standardized math test scores by twenty percent. I promise. It works with conversion (inches to feet, centimeters to yards), cooking (tablespoons to teaspoons, cups to quarts), and more.

At 40+, I'm friendlier. I love meeting other authors and readers and making new friends online. I am sometimes a social media butterfly, and I don't care what people think or say about it. I "like" freely and promote others' work with great joy. Through writing, I've gathered new friends from all over the country. My life is much richer for accepting online friendship, especially with those in the adoption community. Imagine messaging for months or years with a mother who waits for a baby, and then one day she tells you, "A birth family chose us! We are going to be parents!"

I'm much less shy in my alone time too. I used to think inside my mind. Now I just go ahead and talk to myself out loud. I'm easier to understand that way. As my grandfather Big Man used to say, "I can't imagine anyone I'd rather talk to than me." Sometimes people at the grocery store interrupt me, though, or try to answer questions I ask myself. So rude.

Theory 27: Orthopedic bras ain't sexy.

A friend's daddy once joked that "pale blondes with big breasts are more fun in the dark." For him? Yes. His burdened wife? No. I can vouch. Though 40+ is the perfect age, body parts post 40 lag, sag, bag, and threaten to turn me all hag. I considered writing an entire chapter titled "My body in spring" because, like Amerigo Vespucci, I find new worlds and landforms during what Alaskans call the break up. I also thought of writing a Theory titled, "Nature's first green ain't gold; it's a blue varicose vein." You don't really know how much weight you packed on during the winter until you put on your shorts, then worse, your bathing suit, and, God help us all, your bathing suit in a hotel room. Over the last ten years, my muffin top expanded from Entenmann's Little Bites to Otis Spunkmeyer. Can I still call it a muffin top if sits under my armpits? My swimsuit looks the same in the back as it does on the front. By 2021 I'll be wearing sleeves all summer. Now I understand why old ladies cover their arms in aggravating linen. Ugh. There are tricks, of course, to make you look better: dark fabric, vertical lines, compression underwear, wire, and skinny mirrors. The best are the five-dollar dorm door mirrors at Walmart. You're welcome. Some things look better standing up than lying down. Now I understand black-out curtains. Luckily, Tall Child's eyesight is fading at about the same rate as my beauty. Anyway, along with all those tricks, some of us require support, as in *orthopedic* equipment. I wrote about how "well-endowed" girls suffer harassment and are often misunderstood in "Theory 6: Don't judge a woman by her accent or her breast size."

I nickname everyone and everything. My "girls?" Of course, I named them! They are part of my being, my history, my personality, my struggles and triumphs, and personal topography. Thus, they are named Atlantic and Pacific (referred to here as A and P). These names give merit to their vastness, their weight, their volume, and the fact that that they're impossible to harness. And, I mean HARNESS. That's what big breast bras feel like: over-the-shoulder-boulder-holders that are NEVER comfortable. Just the words for the components sound awful: boning, straps, wire, netting, hooks and eyes, spiral metal, extenders, and separators. And those are *modern* terms. Our poor ancestors. My roots are English and Scots-Irish. If I had lived back then, I probably would have been a poteen-pouring shebeen waitress with drunken gropers driving me nuts. I sympathize with any woman with huge breasts and no access to a sturdy, comfortable bra.

I've coped with A and P since they budded around 1984. I had a role model, as I grew up in the sweet shadow of my hero Dolly Parton. We come from the same town: Sevierville, Tennessee. I've met her. Once, when my cousin and I played on the Catons Chapel Elementary School playground, Dolly's daddy walked by (he lived down the road), talked with us, and gave each of us a quarter. I went to school with Dolly's niece and nephew. Dolly and I played instruments in our high school marching bands. We have similar personalities and attributes. We're writers. We're salt-of-the earth. We tell it like it is. We wear a lot of makeup. We possess mountain woman sensibility and independence.

Anyway, every few years I work up the nerve to shop for a new bra. Bra shopping is awful, especially when you want to feel pretty but wear orthopedic underwear. Once, when I was on an exercise kick, I searched for a sports bra. The department store sales lady called me "honey"—all sales ladies eventually call me "honey"—as she raked through racks to address my rack. Finally, she proudly exclaimed. "I think this one will work! The material was engineered by NASA!" No joke. NASA was credited on the label. I bought it and wore it OVER my regular bra as I paced Lakeshore Park's two-mile path and worked in my yard. Ever raked in a life jacket? Try it sometime. Speaking of life jackets, I can't zip them. I'm better off looping my arms through the nylon straps of a boat seat cushion to resemble an albino sea turtle.

Swimsuit shopping is its own special dose of [you know]. I promise you, those labels that say *D* are cruel, expensive bait for my manatees. Once, in Panama City Beach, Delicious took me to a massive neon shop whose sign assured, "1,000,000 swimsuits" and something like "a swimsuit for everyone." I followed Delicious into that shop with confidence and, after dozens of humiliating attempts to marshal my mallows, I collapsed behind the little dressing room curtain in silent tears. I was young then. Now that I'm 45, I don't really bother. I find the biggest, most expensive black suit Land's

End sells and squeeze into it. It's hot. Then I cover cleavage with a draping coverup. Hot. Once, my buddy Lifestar convinced me to accompany her to the swimsuit section of Dillard's. She's tough, genuine, and 100 percent authentic. On top of all that, Lifestar is a shopping genius—efficient, frugal, and <u>fashionable</u>. She would NEVER wear Crocs and Capri's. I usually shop alone. I don't like to change in front of other women, and ever since I saw the Webb swim team naked all at the same time, I have despised locker rooms. People are always patronizing, "Oh, your boobs don't look *that* big to me." That's because I wear undercover harnesses and "squeezers" (Red Hot's daughter Suspenders' term for tight-fitting camisoles). I knew even Lifestar couldn't find me a bathing suit, so my goal at Dillard's that day was to make sure she at least got a good show for her kind efforts.

~~~

Flashback: Delicious once donned a new navy and turquoise swirled one-piece with a sort of apron that swept across her privates and thighs. Unlike most chunky ladies, Delicious LOVES to go to the women's department and try on plus-size clothes. She modeled for me, turned sideways, and asked, "Bug, tell the truth. What do I look like in this bathing suit?"

I said, "A capital *D*."

~~~

All right, back to the "Bug and Lifestar Seek a Swimsuit Show."

Saleslady: "May I help you?"

Bug, loudly, for all to hear: "YES! I want to try on the biggest booby swimsuits you have. All of them! I wear a 34J. That's FOUR D's, an E, an F, a G, an H, and a J. There's no *I* in bra! Do you have any 34J bathing suits with skirts or board shorts hooked on? Can you find me something colorful? Why are all the big girl swimsuits black or blue? Why can't we wear yellow or red? That's color-ism or fat-ism or boob-ism, don't you think?"

Lifestar and the sales rep took all that as a challenge. They brought me suits that they just KNEW would fit. I put them on and

71

watched in delight (I love being right) as they gasped. Spatial reasoning is crucial when selecting swimsuits to cover large ground. I did some spirited jumping jacks and ran in place for a bit to show Lifestar just how hard my boob-life is. Lifestar found one TANKini that came close. The colorful blue, black, and---yippee---brown and pink suit did cover, but the support was minimal. I bought the top. Swimsuit bottoms bother me. I think I have a sensory problem. If my waistband is tight, I can't concentrate, so I wear shiny black compression underwear-girdles that rise high to my bra line and smooth out the bumps from there to my rear. Comfortable? Not really, but remember my bras are vices with no stretching and lots of rods and wires. I feel exposed if I'm not bound like a Geisha. Why don't manufacturers don't build suits *around* bras. Why can't the sales lady say, "Here are all the 34J swimsuits, honey." I hoped Jessica Simpson would jump on that, but she let me down.

During the summer of 2014, I wore a swimsuit four times. Heck, just the process of stretching a Miracle Suit over my body is a nightmare that requires the following tools:

Privacy
Elbow room (Yes, I have punched myself in the eye.)
Cornstarch
Something to look forward to

Even at Disneyworld, where tourists whose cultures ignore the merits of deodorant and razors surrounded me and I should have felt pretty, I felt gross.

Mini-Theory: If you can afford to fly from Europe to America for a family vacation at Disneyworld, you can certainly afford Ban Roll-On.

When we scheduled the trip, I freaked when I realized I had to visit Typhoon Lagoon. I had two choices. 1) I could wear shorts and a T-shirt and look like a holy roller. You know those girls with long hair who wear foundation makeup but no blush or mascara, scuffle around in heavy denim skirts, and play basketball in skorts? Do you love how they stand out but their husbands blend right in with all the other guys? 2) I could suck it up, batten down the hatches, and physically participate in Sharky's life.

You see, we visited Disneyworld with Sharky's *baseball team.* The boys were eleven and twelve. They'd all seen the school video "Changes," but I didn't think they were ready to go eye-to-eye with Atlantic and Pacific. Not yet. One of Sharky's basketball teammates had told him, "Your mama is hot." I never should have bought him those Skittles. He totally got the wrong idea.

In Orlando, where a secret equator that's more grid than circle steams up parking lots and turns underwire bras into cattle branding irons, I had an epiphany. I thought, *Bug, wear your bra under your swimsuit.* I had a swimsuit that was black and brown with wide straps that covered my bra. Great! My girls were contained and concealed, and Sharky's teammates saw no cleavage. They battled the wave pool in innocence without being visually assaulted by my Mountain Oceans. The only problem happened late that night when I couldn't find my bra. Tall Child and I tore apart Room 305 of Caribbean Beach Resort looking for it until I realized I had it on under my swimsuit. I had forgotten. My bras are as valuable and irreplaceable to me as my wedding ring, but I have to take the bras off and am always uneasy when I can't quickly locate them.

Here's the deal. Big breasts are HEAVY. They are much heavier than fat. The straps, no matter how wide, work grooves into your shoulders. The grooves left by bra straps are pinkish red, permanent indentions with obvious ridges, or as we say in the hollers, banks. And sweat collects there. In summer, there's a sweat flood. Think *A River Runs Through It.* So, let's call my not-so-groovy grooves "Tennessee" and "Mississippi."

Tote that barge,
lift that bale,
wear my bra,
and you'll think you're in jail.

Get the picture? Maybe I should get shoulder tattoos of my boys fishing off the banks and holding cane poles. Gnome on one shoulder, Sharky on the other?

I hope I've adequately established how painful, humiliating, expensive, and typically hopeless bra shopping was for me, until the Classy Lady ladies told me about "The Bra Lady" in Fountain City.

Once, I had to go to a fancy party that Dogwood Deb co-chaired. I was happy to support her loving, tireless fundraiser efforts, but I was worried sick about one monumental task: finding a formal dress that modestly covered and held up my "top" for under $200, in under two weeks' time. Delicious and I literally visited <u>every</u> formal dress shop in Knoxville, Tennessee. At every shop, I heard and saw myself (you know, like in an out-of-body-experience) say to the workers, "Y'all don't understand. Big breasts are heavy. Please don't tell me to 'just wear a strapless bra.' If a NASA sports bar with two-inch-wide straps doesn't cut the mustard, what on earth [pun intended] makes you think a strapless Playtex design can?" In a last-ditch effort visit to an old Knoxville standby fancy shop, Classy Lady, a miracle occurred. A hot pink FUSCHIA dress with a wide, layered, floor length skirt magically appeared. The dress was loud, but its levies channeled Atlantic and Pacific with adequate modesty. For $150. Miracle on 34J street!

After hearing my woes and receiving my unending gratitude for finding me a dress that fit and that I could afford, the Classy Lady clerk advised, "Honey, I think you should go see the bra lady up between Halls and Fountain City."

"What? Who's that?" I asked.

All the clerks circled around me. They nodded, smiled as though "There's hope for you yet" was tattooed on their foreheads, and practically chanted:

Bra Lady, Bra Lady,
Fountain City, Halls.
She can work magic,
With your bowling balls!

The Classy Lady woman handed me a pale pink homemade business card. For the first time in a long time, I saw a light at the end of two long tunnels. Just holding The Bra Lady's business card in my hand, I perked up. And, her name is *perfect*.

I feel another Theory coming on: *God names people for their life missions.* It's not an original idea, I'm sure. I read Lois Lowry. In the third book of *The Giver* series, *The Messenger,* main character

Matty's futuristic, yet primitive society gives villagers "True Names" based on their spiritual, academic, artistic, or physical giftedness. I couldn't nickname the bra lady better if I tried.

The bra lady's real name indicates providence, divine intervention, a "bigger plan." Her name is………her name is……..drum roll……………………………….her name is………… Illa Brawdy! Yep. **BRA**wdy. *BRA* is in her name! How about that? And, how about that first name, "Illa?" She's the only Illa I've ever met. She is unique. Plus, BRAwdy is her married name. Do you think she was so hell-bent on a career of harnessing women parts that she pursued Mr. Brawdy for his surname, or, do you think the romantic stars aligned so that big-busted women of East Tennessee could remember who to call if they lost that promising pale pink business card? I phoned her. Her aged, honeysuckled voice reassured me. I couldn't wait for relief!

Finally, the day came. Sharky was with me. We drove north to Fountain City and pulled off a busy main road and up a steep driveway into Illa Brawdy's place of business, B & G Shop. I think the letters stand for Brassiere and Girdle, which may indicate her business's founding date. Mrs. Brawdy fashioned a business out of her basement. Cats greeted Sharky and me as we opened the door. Mrs. Brawdy instructed Sharky, "Go pet the kitty-cats while I help your mama."

I instantly recognized I was in the presence of greatness. Can't you just sense it when you are with someone who is exceptional at something? Mrs. Brawdy is to bras as Dolly Parton is to song-writing. Mrs. Brawdy is to bra-fitting as Agape Agave is to margarita-mixing. I wanted her to rock me in her basement rocking chair and tell me everything would be all right. I completely trusted her on sight. She had blonde, sprayed curls, plastic-picked to perfection atop her head. She wore a thin, dressy blouse tucked into slacks with a wide belt cinching her petite frame. Her breasts shot straight out, parallel to the linoleum.

Mrs. Brawdy took me behind a homemade curtain to a tiny room and whipped a measuring tape out of thin air. Her aged-thin hands fluttered across my chest in a mathematical, mumbling fury. She measured, jotted numbers onto index cards, measured, jotted, measured, jotted. Then she announced, "Okay, let's try on some bras! What do you need your bra to do?"

It was like the best psychiatrist ever had just said, "You get unlimited sessions for free. Tell me about your marriage."

I breathed back tears and said, "I need support. My breasts are much heavier than they look. My shoulders and neck hurt. I want the back band to stay put. I want to minimize without pain."

Mrs. Brawdy said, "All righty. I have JUST the bra that will do that job!" She left me hanging for a bit, and then returned with a beige get-up and explained, "Okay, dear, this will do the trick."

I looked at the thing and said, "It doesn't have underwire. I need wire."

She explained, "No, you don't, you just need a well-made bra. This here is a suspension bra. It is made so that all the work and weight are balanced throughout the garment. Right now, your poor shoulders are doing all the work. That's why your neck hurts and you have the indentions. Trust me."

Honest to God. I quickly realized I needed help to put the thing on. There I stood, in a closet in Fountain City, surrounded by cats and curtains and baskets of bras as soap operas played on the basement den TV, when the elderly expert Illa Brawdy asked, "Sweetheart, do you mind if I touch your breasts?"

"I don't mind."

Like a sick, sleepy child in need of a nightgown, I stuck my arms into the air and let her dress me. She slid the straps over my arms and scurried around to my back side. She instructed, "Okay, hold this back clasp together for me." She scurried around to my front side. She literally picked up Atlantic and dropped her into her new cup home. She then picked up Pacific and dropped her into her new cup home. Plop, plop. She clasped the back and said, "Now, bend over and jiggle to get things in place." I bent and jiggled. She stuffed, tucked, and tugged. She said, "Turn around and look in the mirror. What do you think?"

Well, in one fitting, I'd gone from soft serve in large cups to vanilla scoops in sugar cones. Wow! I'll give Brawdy this much: I appeared twenty pounds lighter and ten years younger in that bra. I looked in the mirror and said, "I look just like a lady named [PF Classic] I grew up with. So funny!"

Brawdy excitedly said, "Yes you do, because she's my client and this is the exact same bra and SIZE that she wears! What a neat coincidence."

My humored heart sank. That wasn't my goal. PF Classic was close to 70 years old, and while she looked great, I was in my early thirties and wanted modern boobs, not classic ones. Though I felt fancy FREE (the suspension bra was awesome), I was disappointed. A and P looked like something engineered at Oak Ridge National Laboratory. I could lie on Interstate 40 in place of two orange cones. I wanted soft, rounded breasts that were high and perky and sexy. The Golden Gate Bridge bra covered every millimeter of my breasts. I voiced my concern to Brawdy.

She said, "Sweetheart, you need different bras for different *situations*." Here came the cross-sell. She continued, "This is your working girl bra. You wear this when you need support for long hours and want to look thin and fit."

I said, "Well, do you have anything, um, younger-ish?"

She said, "Oh, so you want a little sugar showing? Okay. Let's find you a romantic piece."

Back to the bins she went. One hour and $140 later, I left, exhausted and sore, with Golden Gate and a black T-shirt bra and a new sense of confident freedom. But, that didn't last long. Once I got out of The Bra Lady's basement and out from under her spell, I felt super self-conscious in the Golden Gate. Now I use it as a stage prop during book signings.

~~~

Delicious, years ago, spotted a diamond in the rough bins at Dillard's—a gem of a bra, manufactured in France. She found the prize egg, really, a 34DDDD Chantelle bra that not only fit me, but also minimized me. I kept the bra's tags in my wallet with other irreplaceable papers (teaching license, adoption approval letter, Delicious's prescription list). Since then, I've ordered those bras online. Online shopping for lingerie in my size is utilitarian and efficient. But, in 2014, my cups overflowed to the breaking point.

One November Saturday, as I cleaned ketchup off Gnome's bedroom wall, I grazed an old nail sticking out of the plaster and ripped a hole in Pacific's French, $90 black lace cup. The levy broke. Think buttered biscuits in a minnow trap. I thought, *Great. More expense at the most expensive time of year. Yay me.* I informed Tall Child that he was financing a new dam/bra/trap for me as a

Christmas present. I huffed and puffed and searched through cyberspace only to be met by a grievous realization; like all perfect lipstick shades or diet foods that taste good and work, my Chantelle style was discontinued. Tragic. Now I had to go on a physical search and locate a new bra. Double miserable whammy. Duct tape and winter layers got me through Christmas. Finally, on a rare February weekend morning when Sharky had no basketball ballgames, I ventured out to the mall for a bra hunt.

Two hours and 70 attempts later, I left with a $68 34H that barely fit and had an epiphany. It was time to partially say goodbye to A and P. I'd hit the ocean wall. The following Monday, I called a plastic surgeon and set an appointment to discuss breast reduction. I told Agape Agave about it, and she said, "Oh, no, Bug, this makes me sad. You are our personal Dolly." A and P were a huge part of my identity. But I hurt. I was weary. I was ready to lay down that load. I scheduled the surgery and anticipated it with nervous apprehension. Would I freak out and feel like parts of me were missing? I would no longer have my number one excuse for not exercising and not wearing a bathing suit. Folks would no longer compare me to my hero.

Did I have the guts for *elective* surgery? Yes! I scheduled the surgery for my school Christmas break, for two reasons. 1. I'd have plenty of teacher time off to recover, and 2. I figured doing the surgery at Christmas would be par for the yucky, pressure-filled, seasonal course. I had it all figured out . . . .

Theory 28: Working mothers are the man.

Working mothers know plans are pointless. Right? JUST when you have everything mapped out to save money, accomplish goals, raise decent children, step up the career ladder, and be a better wife, all hell breaks loose. And, doesn't it seem like EVERYTHING happens at once? I was busy as I anticipated my Christmas breast reduction and had so many "big" things going on that I had to make a list and tape it to my computer.

- A four-hour breast reduction surgery and three weeks of recuperation.
- With Red Hot, edit, format, proofread, upload, order, proof, revise, order, proof, finalize, plan a launch party, do the whole permission slip and parent order form blitz, and more for a HUGE poetry anthology project with 470 freshmen authors.
- Finish master's degree in curriculum and instruction.
- Continue secret mission to find and buy an old cabin near Little River in Townsend, Tennessee, with no down payment and no extra money for a mortgage.
- Figure out a way to pay for private school. Explanation: Sharky, who has a hearing deficit in his left ear, needed to go to a smaller, quieter school instead of the big, loud middle school for which he was zoned. For many years, we thought a relative was going to pay for the schooling, but two weeks into Sharky's sixth grade year, we realized that was incorrect. Tall Child couldn't leave his good job. My teacher paycheck wasn't enough. I LOVED teaching school. I did NOT want to quit. Sharky was enrolled, on the basketball team, and happy, so Tall Child and I were in a pickle.

I talked with my principal about the private school tuition situation. I said, "I am basically the proverbial man." I am "the woman" whose job must not only provide a good income, but must also provide health insurance, dental insurance, vision insurance, and retirement benefits. As Pearl puts it, "I'm the he-she, the him-her, the she-shim, the shim-sher." Please note that I honor and respect Tall Child. He works very hard and has top-notch employers and clients. I'm proud of him, but we are a two-person (actually, we need three persons) income situation. I was only a third-year teacher and could go back into banking to earn more. The path was obvious, but sad. I would miss all those holiday and summer weeks off with Sharky and Gnome.

I figure I'll get some housewife panties in a wad over the next few paragraphs. Yes, it is tiring taking care of children all day. Babies are boring. I know. I was a housewife for a short stint when Sharky was ages three to five. But, working mothers are The Man. And working *single* mothers are The Super Man. Once, when Sharky was a baby, and I was a full-time banker working nine hours a day Monday-Friday, every fourth Saturday, and every other Thursday night, with only two weeks of annual vacation, Tall Child smarted off, "This house is a wreck. [Friend's stay-at-home wife] keeps her house clean and smelling good all the time."

At that exact moment, I was digging through my top dresser drawer for comfortable underwear. I immediately abandoned my panty search and wrapped my fingers around the drawer's two handles. With Olympic discus throwing power, I jerked that drawer out of the dresser in one fluid motion. My execution was so swift that my granny panties and boulder holders stayed put until the drawer slammed and broke against my closet door on the other side of the bedroom. I think that's called centrifugal force—that physics concept that keeps your back to the wall on the county fair tilt-a-whirl. Tall Child deftly dodged the flying rectangular saucer and said, "I'm not fixing that."

"Of course, YOU aren't fixing it," I screamed, "I'm the he-she, the him-her, the she-shim, the shim-sher. I'll get *my* wood glue out of *my* tool box and fix it!"

"You are psycho."

"Yep, but I can fix a drawer with wood glue."

I think if my boobs hadn't been so big, that drawer would have hit him. They threw off my rotation. You don't see many female Olympic athletes in 34D or higher bras. Not long ago, Tall Child and I cruised through town in my car during a half-marathon. I told him, "Watch. You'll see all the girls with big boobs at the end of the race." I also told him, "Middle-aged working mothers are fat because if we take a walk, everybody pouts until we return. Heaven forbid I be so selfish as to leave my house at night to exercise when y'all are hungry."

Back to my daring diatribe. Being a housewife was *profoundly* easier than being a working mother. As my hard-working, dynamo sister-in-law Dogwood Debutante said after I griped about Tall Child's thoughtless remark, "Wow, my house would be clean too, if I had an extra *50* hours a week at home!"

Boobs, work, temper tantrums, master's degree, Christmas approaching, secret house-buying with no money . . . I was overwhelmed. Good news (ish) finally came! I snagged a job with my old bank. I called my doctor and begged him to move my surgery date up. I would start the bank job December 1. As a new/re-hire, I couldn't take two weeks off for months, and did NOT want to postpone the breast reduction. The doctor worked it out.

On the morning of October 1, I checked into the hospital a whopping, strap-straining, back-aching size 34J. Late that night, I checked out of the hospital a few pounds lighter and eight, yes, **E-I-G-H-T** cup sizes smaller. Think proportional reasoning, or maybe an analogy: 34J is to 34DD as watermelons are to oranges. Getting Atlantic and Pacific reduced and out of my way has changed the speed at which I operate. Burdens were lifted. I can mop faster, reach higher, and high five without bumping boobs with the other high fiver. I can pout better because I can now cross my arms! I wore a bra for the first time in 1984 (fourth grade). For the first month after the surgery, I refused to put one on. I'm no exercise queen, but even today, I opt for a Walmart sports bra. My bullet list shrank too.

- **The Student Anthology Project.** Red Hot Backspace and I finished the anthology and students ordered their copies. The entire school celebrated with a book launch party. School board representatives attended, and the local newspaper features editor wrote a huge spread about our semester-long, real-world, professional project. I couldn't attend the party. I had already started the bank job, and a meeting conflicted with the launch party. It would have been emotionally painful to attend, anyway. I miss that school even now.

- **Job change.** My old University of Tennessee accounting teacher said, "If you are ever in trouble at work, just say, 'I did what I thought was right at the time.'" Perhaps it was a mistake to leave teaching and return to banking, but I did what I thought was right at the time. It's funny that, as I grieved my decision aloud, women always challenged me, asking, "How will this impact Sharky and Gnome? How can you work that schedule AND **take care** of them?" Ironically, the men said, "This is a no-brainer. You have to **take care** of your family. Take the bank job." I wondered, *How can I ever say goodbye to my work sister-wife Red Hot Backspace?* I also had to divorce my work boyfriend Sugar Bear. At least the separation was easy for him. He didn't know we were dating. In addition to all the above stress . . .

- **Master's Degree.** I sat in one hard chair for four straight hours to articulate my teaching philosophy. Why did it matter? I was a banker again.

Redneck goober-toter

- **Delicious and I found a house in the mountains near Little River and bought it behind Tall Child's back.**

Grandmama Buddy used to console Delicious after one of her earring splurges, "Delicious, what's the point of working like a dog if you never have anything to show for it?" I had worked like a dog all but two years since I was fifteen years old. Delicious worked like a dog as a high school English teacher and summer waitress from age eighteen until retirement and continues to proofread for me and substitute teach at Sevier County High School. Maybe, like men, we needed something to show for all of our work. When men find work success, they think they deserve better cars. They waste money on boats that constantly break down. Some acquire expensive secret girlfriends and end up in expensive public divorces. Many women, however, feel guilty for spending money on themselves. Delicious and I decided to think like men, but we had only one problem. Yes, we'd worked hard and found professional success, but, because all our modest teacher income went to fund family life and educations, we had no extra money to bankroll our dream. That said, we *never* factor the lack of money into our dreams. Why would we? When we dream, we pray and work. And we usually see our dreams come to fruition, often to the amazement of others. When I applied to become an adoptive mother, I was in the middle of graduate school and at the bottom of the recession with $300 in my checking account. I gave the adoption agency $100 of it. Every time I went to the grocery store, I bought diapers. Two years later, I was thankfully putting them on baby Gnome.

This is how the whole thing went down. For an entire summer, Tall Child repeatedly watched Delicious and me back out of the driveway and cruise over to Townsend for the day. He would say, "You two are nuts. What are you doing?"

One of us would say, "Tall Child, we are looking for a house over near Little River."

He'd say, "Okay, girls. Have fun with your pipe dream. How would you even pay for it?"

I'd say, "Money is irrelevant. We'll figure that out later. Don't underestimate us." Then, we'd laugh our a$$es off as we house-hunted with only enough spare money to buy fountain Cokes and hot dogs at the Phillips 66 gas station on the way home.

Our search was somewhat unconventional, I suppose. We basically drove or walked through the neighborhoods that hug

Little River. We put notes on doors, trespassed like crazy, and talked to locals. By the way, if a screen door sports a padlock, you can still get into the house. Simply unscrew the whole contraption, door handle and all. Do NOT drop the screws in the grass. One day, in our favorite neighborhood, Delicious and I waved hello to a man as he grilled supper on his second-story deck. Delicious yelled up to him, "Hey! We are looking to buy a house here, but we need a cheap one because we're both teachers."

The man said, "Hang on. I'm coming down there." We introduced ourselves, and he said, "You can forget about any of these houses on the river. You can't afford them, and no one will sell, but I might be selling an old place I own in October."

"Really? Where is it?"

The guy, Jacksonville Junker, was blunt. He continued, "It's that black house between the two white ones. I can't show it to you, because I have renters. They are filthy. Everyone in the neighborhood is mad at me for renting to them, so I'm trying to kick them out. If I do, you're welcome to look at the place." BINGO! I got his number and called him in October. We drove by countless times but couldn't get a good look. Finally, we met a neighbor who let us in to see the old cabin once the renters had been evicted. As Delicious and I waded through the renters' garbage, envisioned repairs and improvements, and got excited, we remembered we had no actual money. Still, I said, "We want it."

Mama and I schemed, prayed, and wondered where we'd get the money and if Jacksonville Junker would owner finance. You see, the house would NEVER pass inspection for financing. The only insulation on the house was a pink square in the basement, which I removed it because it was holding a crunchy dead bat carcass.

The next week, I got a letter from the bank from when I worked there in 2004. It said I could liquidate my old 401K and get a whopping $4,900. Not long after that, Delicious's cousin asked if she could buy her out of a little jointly-owned acreage in Wise, Virginia. I think Delicious got about $5,000. We told Jacksonville Junker that we wanted to make an offer.

We had $9,500 to put down. His price? $69,500.

He said, "Well, Bug, if you can pay Delicious's half when she dies, and you two promise to pay my children when I die, I'll finance it for 30 years. Can you put ten percent down?"

OF COURSE, WE COULD! We shook on it right there as we stood on top of three layers of linoleum in a kitchen with a plywood ceiling.

October 31, Delicious and I sneaked off to a lawyer's office in Knoxville to sign mortgage papers. We closed. We bought a 1956 cabin, which cost about what a nice new car costs (not that I've ever bought a *new* car), about 100 steps from Little River in Townsend, Tennessee. The timing was nerve-wracking for two reasons. 1) I was still a teacher and negotiating with the bank. I wasn't sure what salary they would agree to. I had to make enough extra (compared to teaching) to pay Sharky's tuition and now half the cabin mortgage. 2) Tall Child had no clue. After we signed all the papers, the closing attorney said, "I bet your husband is excited to fish that river and spend the weekend in his own cabin."

I said, "He doesn't know about it yet."

Both men went down, belly-laughing and wishing me luck. The lawyer said that in decades of practice, he'd never met a spouse who bought a house without telling his/her partner. I told him, "My husband would have talked me out of this, and I didn't want to be talked out of my dream. He'll be okay, I think, as long as I find a way to make the payments."

Mama named our cabin Riverdance.

On the way home I bought a postcard of a Smoky Mountain black bear and stapled it to a bag full of Halloween candy. I gave the treat to Tall Child. I instructed him to read the back of the postcard, where I'd written, "Congratulations! You are now the proud owner of an old house near Little River. I can't wait to have all kinds of adventures with you, Sharky, and Gnome. I love you." He took it *okay*. Whew. He must know the "Seventy times seven" thing.

Delicious, Gnome, and I spent our first night at Riverdance November 1. We happily cleaned and froze in 29-degree mountain air as we laughed in shock at our risky behavior. Good times. I was still so preoccupied with my potential job change that I couldn't really "let loose" until the following Monday. Sunday night, I called in sick to the school substitute hotline, so I had Monday off to work on Riverdance with Delicious. We were about to go home Monday afternoon and decided to take a walk along the river to the historic swinging bridge on Walnut Loop in Sunshine Unincorporated (speed limit ten). Gnome threw rocks in the river and Delicious prattled on as we walked onto the bridge.

My cell phone rang. On the line was the human resources recruiter for the bank. He asked, "Are you somewhere you can talk?"

I laughed, "Yes, I am. Actually, I am standing in the center of the swinging bridge over the Little River in Townsend."

He cast his line. I swallowed the hook. You see, I'm a Christian. Christians see things. Wasn't it obvious, from all the surroundings and timing, that I should say "yes" to the bank's offer?

Don't you think it's meant to be, since the branch I would manage is called the Walland Branch and that it is only fourteen minutes from Riverdance? Oh, and the address for Riverdance is Old *Walland* Highway? As Pearl might say, "How about THAT? That is that. Done!"

I bought the house Friday, October 31. I secured the job that would help pay for it Monday, November 3. I was The Man. I left a job I LOVED and returned to banking to take care of business. As I anticipated Day One of my new (old) job, I wondered if I'd made the right call. I'd seen signs of promise and peace, but the final solace, the final "yes" I needed, came from my awesome friend. That shining moment of sureness followed tumultuous weeks. On December 1 at 9:00 a.m., I checked in at the human resources desk, and my new boss took me on a tour of the building (the main office where all line of business partners work). We took the elevator to the serious third floor executive offices. We politely greeted and visited our way down the corridor and then walked into the office of my dear old buddy RokNVol. Okay, I can't take credit for her nickname. It's on her license plate. I can't top that nickname, anyway. She is a true Tennessean, a die-hard Vol fan, and got married at a rock concert in Big Orange Country. She won the wedding package on the radio. She's REAL. She gets it. She is The Man.

Anyhow, we stepped into her office and she SCREAMED! She JUMPED! She YELLED, "YAAAAAAAAAAY! BUG IS HEEEEEERE!!!!!!!!!!!"

She was a one-woman, All-Vol spirit tunnel.

I was sick to my stomach on the way to work that morning (sad, nervous, tired), but RokNVol cured me with a perfect dose of friendship. RokNVol, thanks for opening the T for me. I love you for it.

I was sad to leave teaching for many reasons. At school, I laughed all day, but I consoled myself by remembering that crazy stuff goes down in retail bank branches all the time. Retail bankers are like bar tenders who serve money instead of liquor. During my first banking stint from 1995 through 2004, I narrowly escaped getting a beatdown from a rough woman in the drive-through. She didn't have a car, but she had a mission: to cash a forged check or kill me trying. It was so rough in a couple of my branches that we had security guards. Unfortunately, I had to fire one of the guards because he banked with us and bounced checks constantly. He asked me, "What's the big deal?"

I explained, "You have severe financial problems. And a gun. And you stand beside a vault all day, which is uncomfortably close to my desk."

I "managed" a 98-year-old employee who thought *she* managed the "CD Department." There was no such department after 1978, but she managed it just the same from the corner of my downtown branch. If I saw one of her "CD customers" come in the door, I had to quickly call her extension. To wake her up.

When I re-entered the corporate world, I told Delicious, "I'm going to ease back into banking. I don't want other bankers to think I'm wild or crazy. I've been writing and teaching since I left, and my mouth sometimes keeps up with my imagination. I'm going to watch everything I say."

She said, "Bug, you can forget that. Impossible. Just be yourself."

True to form, I messed up my second week when I attended a consumer banking summit with 119 of my new colleagues. As I mingled my way to the parking lot, a co-worker asked, "How do I know you?"

I gave my usual response: "Were you in the UT marching band?"

"No," he said.

I said, "Well, Playboy then."

A circle of bystanders laughed. Then I saw my boss in the circle. Oops!

When I made panicked eye contact with him, I begged, "Sorry?"

To my great delight and human resources relief, he responded, "That's why I hired you, Bug."

I thought, *Okay, I can be me here.* During my last few days at the junior high, students would say, "Mrs. Dyer, you'll only be with us [so many] more days." On my last day, a sweet freshmen boy reminded me, "Well, Mrs. Dyer, this is the day."

I replied to him, "Yes. This is the day that our Lord has made. Let us rejoice and be glad in it." The school is rich in Southern Christian culture, yet it is a public school, so references to Jesus Christ are carefully guarded or avoided. But, as the student noted, that was my last day, so I figured I'd take a chance. He smiled.

At that same consumer meeting where I made the Playboy comment, the bank's then area president stood up to make final remarks. He congratulated and thanked and encouraged. Then he said, "This is the day that the Lord has made. Let us rejoice and be glad in it."

I took that God wink to heart, and knew that, as sad as I was to leave teaching, I'd done what was right at the time. I was The Man. Then I got the Zoloft. I couldn't cry. I couldn't laugh hard. But, I got through those huge changes. Jesus, Riverdance, and Zoloft saved me.

Delicious and I cleaned, dusted, painted, pulled up gross flooring and brought Riverdance to life. We scavenged thrift shops and family basements for furniture. Tall Child's reaction turned from surprise to worry. He never asked to see the house. Months later, I found out why. I asked, "Do you want to go see Riverdance?"

He said, "I looked at it few weeks ago when I was doing work near there. I just saw the outside. Bug, I hope you know what you are doing. I don't even see how we can all sleep there."

I said, "It's bigger than it looks from the outside. Don't worry. You'll have a blast once we get it fixed up."

In February, two huge trees fell through, yes, THROUGH, the house. The insurance and reconstruction process delayed our getting to enjoy Riverdance. Bad luck? Yes. But, the contractors, led by my competent cousin, thusly tagged Property Brother, used the bad luck to improve the cabin overall. Delicious's bedroom floor is now level and her buckled paneling is now clean drywall. We got all new plywood floors in the living room. We painted the floors blue. The winter weather forced us to shut down operations and drain the pipes. We had to wait until after the last freeze to open the cabin. Finally, spring came, and finally, we were out of "before" mode and ready to reveal our dream to the world, starting with the doubting Tall Child. He drove us down Old Walland Highway as I directed. Then he said, as we passed a tiny green box of a house perched right on the edge of the highway, "Where do I park?"

I said, "In the driveway."

He said, "Where?"

I said, "Huh?"

He said, "Isn't that the house?" and looked over at the green box of mildew.

"No! Our house is up there on the right."

No wonder he fretted so much. He thought we'd bought a 500 square-foot house that clung to the bottom of a steep mountain and sat right on the road. It had only one parking spot and one bedroom. He dreaded the wrong house for months.

Once Tall Child was over the shock and I made him his first big batch of Saturday at the river Rotel, he embraced Riverdance and found his weekend perch quite relaxing. I left the Walland Branch every Friday at 6:30 and drove straight to our cabin where my family waited. Yes, I missed all the teacher time off with my children and I despised a lot of the bank work, but I made the best of it because, well, working mothers are The Man.

While the job did take care of tuition and the cabin mortgage, I was very much a square peg in a round hole there. I tried to have many great days as a banker. I put all my vocational teaching skills to work for a personal and corporate profit. I tried to coach my staff to be successful and happy in their work. But, all days wouldn't be good. It turned out that my "thinking outside the barn" wasn't ideal for retail bank branch management. It turns out I was supposed to follow corporate processes instead of creating my own. Creatives and cubicles don't jive. Let me explain.

I always thought the little red square button on my corporate bank office telephone read RIS. I always wondered what words stood behind the RIS acronym.

I hit that RIS button at 4:40 p.m. on Monday, May 8, 2017, to end my attachment to that day's conference call. Immediately, the other line rang. And rang. And rang. I answered, hoping the conversation would be quick. It was.

"[Bank], this is Bug, may I help you?"

"Hey Bug, this is Sweet Christmas in human resources. Can you meet Boss Bob and H.R. Bob in the human resources department at 9:30 a.m. tomorrow?"

"I can. Why?"

"I have no idea, Bug. They didn't tell me."

Of course, they don't tell Sweet Christmas anything. God forbid she turn Paul Revere on them and spread helpful info to hardworking East Tennessee bankers. God forbid she comfort anyone. My stomach turned, partly for psychosomatic reasons, and partly from the ulcer my doctor diagnosed only one week before. I searched my memory. *What have I done wrong? Has one of my employees—Adele, Mama Bear, Fire Woman, or Baby Caddy—done something wrong? Is the bank relocating me? Am I about to get...? No. Surely not.*

I called my manager, Boss Bob. Voice mail. I sent him a text. No reply. I called Sweet Christmas and asked for some insight. She said, "I'm sorry this is giving you anxiety."

I said, "Well, they need to find a more gentlemanly way to schedule these types of meetings. It is rude and disrespectful to have me wonder all night why I'm headed to human resources in the morning."

As a bank branch manager, one has limitless opportunities to fail. I had little time to ponder those opportunities, because I had to meet a colleague for supper at El Jimador. That was the perfect time to sink into a salt-rimmed tequila bath, but I had to stay sober and professional. She and I were headed to the library to teach Habitat for Humanity applicants banking and money management basics.

I wrapped up the mentoring session at 8:15 p.m. and drove 45 minutes home. I bathed Gnome, cleaned up the house, watched a TV show with Tall Child, and checked Sharky's grades. I went to bed. I worried.

Tuesday morning, May 9, I took my boys to their schools and drove to the bank's main office parking lot. I called Delicious, who counseled, "Whatever this is, you'll handle it with intellect and poise. Be calm, but don't let them talk down to you. You needed help, and they made excuses."

You see, my little five-person branch was short a head teller for most of my time there. That forced one of the two sales people (Adele and me) to work as a teller for a stretch of time each day. It's a bit difficult to make outbound sales calls on the phone and in person while physically installed behind bullet-resistant glass. Plus, that time in teller windows caused follow-up and paperwork backups in our stated jobs, branch manager and financial services specialist. I hated to but pestered Merlin the Administration Magician to get help when one of my teammates was sick or on vacation. She did her best and now works for Girl Scouts of America. I covered Adele for lunch. Adele covered the tellers for lunch. No one covered me. Forgive me, but doesn't it seem counterproductive and counter intuitive to delegate *up* the chain of command? When I repeatedly communicated the urgent need for help to human resources and upper management, I heard, "Staffing will always be an issue."

Nothing should "always be an issue." Imagine other industries making such a ridiculous excuse. "Bubonic plague will always be an issue." "The King of England will always be an issue." "Boll weevils will always be an issue."

If opposing countries can sign peace treaties, can't banks hire more tellers? Shouldn't executives who make eight times what a teller makes be problem solvers? Why is the undercompensated teller doing all the compensating for the executive's lack of compassion and creativity? Isn't good employee morale profitable?

PEOPLE are everything.

Hire some.

At 9:25 a.m., I rode the elevator to the second floor and waited for the meeting with Boss Bob and H.R. Bob. I waited at least fifteen minutes. Then they small talked me into the office and discussed some type of software for another five minutes. I thought, *Respect my anxiety and my time. Get on with this.*

They got on it with, all right. I heard, "As you know, your branch did not meet fourth quarter incentive sales goals…so you were put on a performance plan…and first quarter your branch missed the minimum incentive plan goal, so we are ending our relationship."

"Ending . . . with me? So, I'm fired?"

"You no longer work for [the bank]. We are letting you go."

Yes, *they* let *me* go. Girls, always let the guy break up with you. That way, he can suffer in doubt and regret for the rest of his life.

I got my A$$ fired! As embarrassing and frightening as the situation was, I found myself completely at peace. Truth be told, my soul wasn't in that job. My soul was in it as much as I could do what I do best: create, teach, befriend, advise, laugh, and write.

As H.R. Bob rambled through his script (banks employ lots of scripts these days) "keys, combos, blah, blah, you can collect unemployment, blah, blah, look for a packet in the mail, blah."

I perked up, thinking, *I don't have to play Frogger down Alcoa Highway today. If they will stop talking, I can eat lunch at home in my rocking chair and watch* Ellen.

Outwardly, I listened and contributed to that great black cloud of a conversation. Inwardly, I silver-lined the whole ridiculous situation.

H.R. Bob said, "Do you have any questions?"

I should have asked, "Why, when my team was struggling to hit minimums, did you send Adele to another branch for two weeks and leave me alone with only two tellers? Why did you write me up for letting a teller use two hours of sick time to go to court instead of half of a vacation day? Why did you write up someone with three degrees because she missed a computer-based test on individual retirement accounts by one day?" Instead, I said, "I find it illogical that someone of my character and integrity is being fired when [unnamed crook at another branch] is still employed here. Really, he's so crooked you fired his *wife*."

The Bobs' chins dropped a little, but they were silent. Boss Bob spoke fewer than ten words in the entire meeting.

I then said, "I have some requests." I proceeded to lobby for my crew: Adele, Mama Bear, Fire Woman, and Baby Caddy. Case by case, I gave specific warnings and implored them to take better care of that little team.

I never stole, cheated, lied, caused a loss, put junk on the books, mistreated anyone, or jeopardized my Christian values. I am proud of how I treated employees, coworkers, and customers. I am proud of how I ran that tiny branch. We didn't meet *incentive plan* minimum goals (by just under four percent), but we were profitable each year and twelve months rolling by nine or ten percent. I think. It's hard to know exactly because the bank saves money by using Size 4 Calibri font on reports.

My reputation is intact. If I had something to hide, I certainly wouldn't write this Theory.

Boss Bob said he would go to my branch that afternoon to tell my staff. I said, "I'll call them."

H. R. Bob said, "Bank policy requires that your supervisor inform associates in this situation. Also, Boss Bob will clean out your desk, box everything up, and bring it here to The Capitol for you to pick up. That's the policy."

Um, no. I didn't give a flip about their rules. I spent 40 hours a week for three straight years with my team. Not to tell them myself would be rude and weak. *Policy* meant nothing to me. I was "no longer with the bank." I left.

Once I cleared the parking lot, I called Tall Child. "I got fired."

"What?!? Wow. I can't believe that."

"Tall Child, this is terrible. What are we going to do about bills?"

"Oh, you'll land on your feet. You know, this is great timing."

"What?"

"Yes, now you can go to Sharky's and Gnome's end of school stuff. You were going to miss eighth grade graduation, field day, everything."

"Yes, but how about our 50 percent loss in household income that starts now?"

"Meh."

"I think I'll eat lunch with Gnome's kindergarten class tomorrow."

"He will love that. Take May. Help the boys finish out the school year. This time, figure out what YOU want to do."

Reader, in saying "this time," Tall Child referenced my leaving teaching three years prior.

Oddly, or maybe coincidentally, or maybe as it was supposed to be, Sharky and I "graduated" from middle school and banking, respectively, within days of each other. Yes, Tall Child, it was great timing.

Anyway, after I talked with Tall Child, I called my mama. She said, "I am so sorry. They are morons. Will you teach again? This is good, Bug. Now you can write every day."

I said, "I am in shock, but I need to hang up and call my team."

I broke POLICY and called Adele, "I got fired."

"You are joking. Are you joking?"

"Nope. Sales quotas, allegedly. Whatever. I need you to clean out my desk before Boss Bob gets there. He's coming this afternoon. My personal items are none of his business. Box it all up. Make the office look as empty as possible. Be dramatic! Take the pictures off the walls and put them in the closet. I'll come get my stuff later this week."

"I am on it."

On Thursday, Delicious accompanied me to my old branch. I reassured my sweet team, hugged everyone, picked up my stuff, and rode to Riverdance. I mixed a stout Bloody Mary and walked to the swinging bridge over Little River, the exact same place I had stood three years before and accepted that job. Poetic?

If you like Poe, I guess.

As a former educator, I spend loads of time reflecting. After the breakup, I reflected on what I did right, what I did wrong, what I said, what I didn't say . . . you get the picture. I wondered if I was as good a manager as I thought I was and tried my best to be.

Banking has changed. Banking, these days, is retail. *Bankers* have changed. Bankers used to be prestigious community members. They were trusted confidants, advisors, and financial experts. As a modern-day banker, I felt like a telemarketer with all that scripting. My days were planned for me in short blocks of time. I wanted to invest time in people, not processes. I wanted to go on sales calls and see my customers. I was old-school.

I made mistakes. I didn't track numbers. I figured that if I consistently treated people well, and gave them good advice, and gave them TIME to see how that advice worked, they would return to me and bring friends. I put employees' personal lives and professional goals ahead of the bank's. It's not easy managing a bunch of women in tight quarters! See "Theory 39: Men are easier to work with than women."

Corporations don't have souls. People do. I had too much fun at work. I referred to the main office as The Capitol, and my little branch, only 25 minutes from the quiet entrance to the Smoky Mountains, as District 12 from *The Hunger Games*. Maybe one too many times I copied an image of Katniss Everdeen giving her three-finger salute under my corporate email signature. My conference call skills were lacking, to say the least. Now and then, I'd inject humor and creativity or have Adele play Rue's Whistle in the background for all to hear. Conference calls are a cliché exercise in humiliation. They tempt weak employees to embellish, fib, or cheat to avoid embarrassment. I asked my boss one time, "Does the number of checking accounts reported on our daily call determine your mood for the rest of the evening?"

"Yes," he said.

I replied, "Your poor children."

Of all my retail sins, I am most guilty of falling short (numbers-wise) on a daily expectation. I didn't "disposition" enough sales leads. It drove Boss Bob nuts.

Being a writer, I tried to conjugate the word to find more meaning in the task:

The banker dispositions.
The banker is dispositioning.
The banker has dispositioned.
The banker dispositioned.
The banker was dispositioning.
The banker had dispositioned.

You see, kind reader, I couldn't *disposition* leads because *disposition* IS A NOUN. Think of it this way:

The banker nouns.
The banker is nouning.
The banker has nouned.
The banker nouned.
The banker was nouning.
The banker had nouned.

See? For one week, I ignored that cardboard box Mama Bear and Adele packed with all my office junk. When I did finally sort through it I found a severance package! In their furious rush to clean out my office, Adele and Mama Bear threw everything in. I scored a roll of stamps! I got my own home staple remover. I also found an envelope full of cash. No, it didn't come from the vault. It came from my friends at work. We had been on a diet since January. Every Monday, each of us women weighed and measured. When a teammate lost a pound or an inch, he/she put money into our diet jar. Our plan was to tally the results July 1 and give the winner the money. By May 9, we'd lost about 40 pounds and 40 inches. They gave me the money. Wasn't that sweet of them?

I suppose if my employees were comfortable enough to weigh and measure their busts, waists, hips, and thighs in front of me, I did some things right. I'm honored to have worked side by side with Adele, Mama Bear, Fire Woman, and Baby Caddy. I am proud of the work we did together. The episode taught me a few things: My gifts are misplaced in a corporate environment. I was a tie-dyed ink blot splashed on a grayscale Excel spreadsheet. I won't be happy in work unless my tasks match my values. I can absolutely return to teaching, but I want to be my own boss. My whole life, I have revered the written word. My whole life, I have written for release, relaxation, recreation, and reward. I published my first work in 1990. My writing has evolved and served many purposes over time. A few years ago, when I was teaching, I started my small business, Crippled Beagle Publishing. Since the "end of the relationship," I've started dozens of new GOOD relationships and helped many folks realize their dreams of publishing and telling their own stories. God winks at you all the time. Pay attention. No joke; every single time I told someone, "I got fired from the bank," the person responded, "Good. Please tell me you're going to write full time now."

I scribbled out a rough draft of this chapter only eleven days after the bank dumped me. I was at Lakeshore Park's playground with Sharky, Gnome, and Gnome's buddy, The AP. A gentleman who was there with his toddler spoke to The AP and said, "I know your mother."

I recognized him but couldn't place him. I said, "If you know her, I know you. How do I know you?"

We did the whole social dot-to-dot routine, and when he said his wife's name, I said, "YES! I wrote a book about adoption years ago. When you were waiting for your baby, my friend Pearl told me your story. I signed a copy and Pearl gave it to your wife. I hope it helped her."

He spoke through a wide smile, "*That's* who you are."

Amen! *That* is who I am. Little winks and hints over the past decade have formed into a glaring truth. No matter where I've "worked" —from bumper boat girl at The Track to IHOP waitress to banker, teacher, then banker again—I have always, in my heart and free time, been a self-employed writer.

While missing a biweekly company paycheck was terrifying, my ulcer vanished the same week I got fired. One could now describe my ***disposition*** as "engaged and optimistic."

No Bank Job No Cry

I have more time to think, parent, explore, read, drink, watch TV, change light bulbs, you name it. When *you* run your life, you have time to settle curiosities. For example, after much research, I found that the coldest canned Coke in The 9-1-9 can be purchased from a machine at the little gas station across from Sequoyah Presbyterian Church. Also, I Googled "corporate telephone RIS button." I learned that the button reads R*L*S and stands for *RELEASE*. Little did I know when I hit that button at 4:40 p.m., Monday, May 8, that I would never hit it again. Writers do love irony.

Theory 29: College is hard when you're 40.

If you are going to dream big, do it when you are young and less tethered to life's mundane responsibilities. Before you marry and have to think of something to cook for supper every night. Before you have physical impairments. Before you have children to please. I'm just saying that some things are harder at 40 than they are at 20. One example is going to college. Do you have either of these recurring dreams that frequent my wee hours?

1. You've been in school all semester, and it's now time to take the big final exam (one of maybe four grades in the class), and you can't find the testing location. I swear on the Smoky Mountains, in real life back in '94 I failed an Accounting 202 test because I took it in a gigantic theater-seating style room in the Jessie Harris Building at UT. I was a finance major testing in a science building. I credit my awful experience to the intimidating table of elements that stretched wall-to-wall at the bottom front of the depressing room. I am terrible at science. I'm not even sure that it was the Jessie Harris Building. Whatever. I just know that taking the test in an unfamiliar location with 200 other students under the, ugh, letter-number-combos representing matters and gasses mattered to me. I scored an F_2O.

2. The other college nightmare that I often have is that I get notice of a test and realize that I've never actually attended the course. It's too late to withdraw. It's too late to learn. It's even too late to crouch behind the sectional sofa in the athletic dorm and copy down answers from the "tutors" while they help Division One athletes master complex economic theories.

In 1992, I went to college to become a business woman. In 2012, I pursued a post-baccalaureate teacher certification in business education. In 2014, I returned to college to buy myself a teacher raise. That said, I believe education is always good, no matter the reason you seek it. Knowing information, learning skills, mastering and exploring concepts, reading literature, finishing procedures, creating ideas, and performing research illuminate your world forever. When you find a song, read a book, or see a movie that you just love, don't you start to notice references to that song, book, or movie everywhere? Delicious says that people who read poetry enjoy sunsets more than people who don't read poetry. I remember when Ronald Reagan announced his strategic defense initiative and said to military personnel, "May the force be with you." Even as a very young child, I knew *exactly* what he meant because I was "educated" through *Star Wars*. If I'd never seen *Star Wars*, I would have missed the meaning and magnitude and scope of that phrase.

In the late 1940's Jesse Stuart wrote *The Thread That Runs So True*. The book is Stuart's account of his days as a mountain school teacher in rural Kentucky. He makes the following speech to barefoot, poverty-ridden students at Mountain View School:

I told [students] . . . that education was not a commodity to be bought and sold but something that gave one more realization and enjoyment of the many things that life held in store. That with more education, the mysteries and the beauties of life would unfold before them like the buds of leaf and flower in the spring. I told them they would even see more beauty in their natural surroundings than they now saw.

Amen, Jesse Stuart! All this is to say that I place extremely high value on education. Education is the one thing that, once you earn it, no one can take away. It is liberating. I love to learn. I love college-level coursework. I love teaching and teachers. But, I struggled in graduate school because college at age 40 stinks compared to college at age 20. Let's compare the two using Abraham Maslow's Hierarchy of Needs Theory. Shall we? (Educated, self-aware people use the word shall.) I think it's best to start from the basic needs at the bottom and work our way up. Here we go.

Physiological Need: AIR

Bug 1992-1995, ages 18-21: I had just outgrown childhood asthma and could climb the 2.5 million steps on UT's campus with toned marching band legs.

Bug 2014, age 40: I often lost my breath walking uphill from the mailbox and my back hurt when I sat through lectures. Luckily, my grad school classes were held in a converted Food City. There were no stairs.

Physiological Need: FOOD

1992-1995: Meal plan. I took cherry tomatoes from the salad bar to my dorm room and fed them to my secret pet guinea pig Sam. I stole a pineapple from the Presidential Courtyard Cafeteria and soaked it with vodka. I didn't last long at that party. I remember sitting down after dancing quite well and feeling my head bounce on the bar like a bowling ball. At least I was light enough back then to be carried to someone's car.

2014: After working and studying and parenting all week, on Sundays I spent an hour clicking digital coupons, then went to the grocery store to push a heavy cart with apple juice, bacon, milk, loaf bread, bananas, dog food, etc. Then I brought it all home and unloaded it. Then I cooked it. Then I slopped the Hog, Gnome, Sharky, and Buzz. Then I stored leftovers. Then I washed the dishes. Then I put the clean dishes away. Then I read textbooks. On grad school class days, I treated myself to two McDonald's breakfast burritos.

Physiological Need: WATER

1992-1995: Drank it like crazy. Band camp is HOT.

2014: Tried and try to make myself drink it to lose weight. College at age 40 requires lots of caffeine. Water isn't caffeinated.

Physiological Need: SHELTER

1992-1995: I had one half of one room in Humes Hall to clean. Four girls shared a bathroom, and a dorm housekeeper checked our work. I doubt we owned any Comet or Windex. I don't remember sweeping or mopping, but I do remember one big fight about a bar of soap. If we ran out of toilet paper, we just took some from the lobby bathroom.

2014: I will say that signs of my being heavily occupied and the recession show fully in my 1950s rancher. Most of my housework during grad school addressed protecting my computer from Gatorade spills and protecting my papers from becoming a squadron of fighter jets. My repair work was slacking, but I tried. Sharky liked to swing open the fridge door with his body. He'd hold the butter bin and put his little toes on the bottom rail and swing back and forth, banging into the cool contents. The little rails snapped, and our fridge is so old that replacement parts are obsolete. In my recession/expensive grad school/substitute teacher income mode, I got crafty. I bought two, 50-cent wooden yard sticks and Gorilla glued them across the panels. OF COURSE, I placed them with the red measuring markings OUT. That way, if Tall Child asks, "Will you cut me a piece of summer sausage?" I can say, "Sure, how many inches would you like?"

Physiological Need: CLOTHING

1992-1995: Not so good back then. I had two sweatshirts from American Eagle. One had trees all over it and read "Leave nothing but footprints." When I met Tall Child, I wore a buttoned up blouse tucked into blue jeans with no belt. My shoes looked like something from a Tolkien novel. I was 22, living at The Meadows and dressed for The Villages.

2014: Not much better now. Well, teachers' children who become substitute teachers who become teachers who then are forced into uncomfortable banker clothes who then get fired and then become full-time writers shouldn't be expected to be fashionable, right? I refuse to wear underwire unless I have a client meeting. Anyone who has yard sticks holding the mustard back probably won't have scarves, layered necklaces, or silk in her closet. Ironing is for old ladies who use cloth napkins. During grad school classes, I wore Sharky's Sacred Heart sweatshirt over leggings and a tank top, a.k.a., my pajamas from the night before. Um, I have on that EXACT outfit AS I TYPE THIS. Add Sketchers. NO JOKE. I would insert a photo but I have on that Walmart sports bra and yesterday's makeup. Tall Child says he hates leggings, but I don't care. I mean, look around. Women have craved comfort for generations. It's our TIME to be comfortable. Seriously, what if I said to him, "I hate golf shirts." Leggings it is!

Physiological Need: SLEEP

1992-1995: Got it. I could sleep until 11:00 a.m. and stay up past midnight.

2014: Oh, those days were done once Sharky entered the world. Each year I need more and enjoy less. I love to lay out a tasty tailgate spread of measured meats and cheeses on our coffee table, relax into a chair, watch UT kick off, then pass out. But, I rise before the sun and make a ridiculous list of all the things I'll accomplish each day. I'm toast after 5:00 p.m. I have a dilemma too. I WILL exercise, but I need to get it over with first thing in the morning or I won't do it at all. Also, my best time to write is early morning. Also, the best time for me to pay bills or call the IRS is first thing in the morning. During graduate school, I $$$ indulged in caffeine-spiked, mocha coffee drinks from Starbucks.

Physiological Need: SAFETY AND SECURITY

Health

1992-1995: 34-24-34 In infertile retrospect, according to Tall Child, I missed some great opportunities. He says I choked at the buzzer.

2014: When I was teaching and going to graduate school, our school system forced us to weigh in quarterly for a $50 per month insurance discount. My BMI? TMI! I thought I was fat then, but I was twenty pounds lighter than I am now. So, I actually *am* fat now. But, at least in ten years I'll look back on this time and miss being skinny! So, really, I'm skinny now. Yay!

Employment

1992-1995: See the first book's "Theory 9: Everyone should work in a restaurant." I also made telemarketing calls for something like $5 an hour. I dialed, then either hung up on the person or let him/her hang up on me. I wasn't about to harass potential donors.

2014: During grad school, I substitute taught at a few Knox County schools and my church's daycare, then served a tour at a criminal-laden middle school, then caught the leprechaun and taught at wonderfully safe Maryville Junior High. The latter (minus the embarrassing Tennessee teacher pay scale) was a dream job. That said, it's extremely tiring to work all week and go to graduate school all day on Saturdays, especially during SEC football season. Which would you prefer: a group presentation on Chapter 4 of a textbook or a Tennessee vs. Georgia tailgate?

Property

1992-1995: Clarinet, comforter set, lots of the 1928 brand costume jewelry, micro fridge, mechanical pencils, and notebook paper.

2014: See list above and add the second home I can't afford, a Toyota with 250,000 miles on it, my late father-in-law's computer, and paper. Lots of paper.

Family

1992-1995: I was the child and had to take care of no one. Ahhhh.

2014: Delicious, Tall Child, Sharky, Gnome, Buzz (a yapper—may he rest in peace in Heaven), and now Lollipop the cat depend on me. We think a hawk dropped Lolli on The Crippled Beagle Farm. She had a beak-sized hole in her back. Mama played vet and cured her. Tall Child says she brings my blood pressure down. Now she lies behind my computer monitor and swipes at my fingers as I work. I take care of everyone. Well, I try until one of my TV shows comes on. Then I go to bed.

Stability

1992-1995: I enjoyed a true nuclear family, but that fell apart when Pooh died at age 44, in 1993, the summer after my freshman year of college. I regained mental stability within a few years but the remaining years of college were emotionally rough.

2014: In that busy working, parenting, grad school time, I did the best I could with Jesus, anxiety medicine, yard work, and Pinot Grigio.

Physiological Need: LOVE AND BELONGINGNESS

Friendship

1992-1995: Three girls from Gatlinburg. GT, TRO, and Mare were with me from beginning to end. We netted one awesome friend, HH. Funny stuff can happen even when you spend most of your time in a Humes Hall dorm room.

2014: I love people and their flaws, especially crazy and creative ones people who are honest about their flaws. Oddballs abound in teacher education courses. Master's degree classes are a crackpot jackpot!

Intimacy

1992-1995: No way! I was a good little girl. But I did go to band camp. Of course, my college sweetheart's nickname is Nixon Lover. You figure it out.

2014: *Married with Children*.

Connections

1992-1995: No cell phone, no internet, no computer, no social media.

2014: Cell phone (got a smart one in 2014!), internet, social media (a blessing to all only children), and lots of online communities keep me company. This century is so much better than the last one. I totally prefer doing research online at home over trudging through Hodges Library with a roll of quarters it took me two hours of fake telemarketing to earn. I think all children should work in restaurants and be forced to write one paper using a microfiche machine to do the research. That'll put them in their places.

Physiological Need: SELF ESTEEM

Confidence

1992-1995: I had it. I worked fast and turned stuff in on time, but I lost points because I preferred speed over accuracy.

2014: In grad school, I had confidence but was much humbler when writing papers. Also, like other adult learners, everything was on my dime and creating a debt burden, so I asked for help when I struggled. I didn't want to do anything twice.

Achievement

1992: I made decent grades, except in engineering calculus. No hillbilly should ever have a German teacher for calculus. Plus, the class was in the top floor of a building at the top of a million stairs. Concrete climbs and derivatives suck when you're hung over.

2014: I finished graduate school and got a raise. Then I changed jobs, as you know. Then I got fired. Now I write full time and help others write. I recently took on a well-traveled, sophisticated, deeply spiritual client who is SUBSTANTIALLY more intelligent than I am. She hesitated at some of my editing suggestions, but I consoled her, "Look, no matter how much smarter you are than I am, I can still help you. I have an education degree and can *guide* you, even when I don't really know much at all. I perfected this skill while teaching eighth grade math." Education is always a good investment. Shoot, if I hadn't gone to graduate school and made all those teacher friends, I wouldn't know about the guy who posed in the birth announcement with his stripper girlfriend while he was married to my former classmate.

Respect of others

1992: I was protective of my self-esteem and reputation.

2014: I want respect but don't worry about it much because 40+ is the perfect age to not give a flip. In the first class each semester, the professor always asks that trite icebreaker, "What is something no one knows about you?"

My go-to response was, "I am sexually attracted to Mennonite men."

Individuality

1992: I wore lots of white T-shirts and khaki shorts so the band director didn't notice my bloopers.

2014: In college as a grown-up, it's important to just be yourself and be proud that you are awake in an auditorium.

Physiological Need: SELF-ACTUALIZATION

Morality

1992: I was a reasonably good girl and by today's standards, a saint.

2014: I think I was a good wife and mother during those years but working full time and going to college forced me to neglect the family sometimes. I didn't bust up any commandments, though. I mean, you can look at the Mennonite men who live 79.7 miles away in Muddy Pond, Tennessee, but you can't squeeze the sugar cane.

Creativity

1992: It's hard to be creative in finance classes, so I took a writing class.
2014: Graduate school for teachers is all about creativity. Those studies opened my mind to all kinds of methods, like how to use the Rascal Flatts song "Life is a Highway" and erectile dysfunction to teach the concept of realism.

Spontaneity

1992: I couldn't afford spontaneity.

2014: I couldn't afford spontaneity after I bought those coffee drinks.

Acceptance

1992: As my aunt Terrific says of her daughter Bags, I was "often wrong but never in doubt."

2014: Teachers are the best people in the world.

Purpose

1992: I hustled in college to graduate early and save Delicious money.

2014: I hustled in graduate school to earn more money to provide for my family.

Meaning

1992: College was fun for the most part, but once Pooh died, I was there to finish and become employable.

2014: Graduate school had more meaning for me because I was "in the trenches" with fellow educator adults who were bettering themselves and their families.

Inner potential

1992: I did not know my potential, but I listened to Dolly Parton. That's always a good start.

2014: In college as an adult, I learned that your potential increases as you become more educated. I also learned how to recognize potential in students, friends, relationships, coworkers, and so on. Skinny teachers taught me that I could find a good diet and lose weight. Starting Monday.

Bug circa 1992

Bug circa 2014

Theory 30: Women become their mothers, whether they like it or not.

B ack at Gatlinburg-Pittman High School (G-P) I told Delicious, "I want to go to The University of Georgia and major in creative writing."

She said, "What would you do for a living?"

I said, "Write and teach."

She said in the kindest way possible, "I forbid you to become a teacher. You'll never have a dime. I majored in journalism at Georgia, but when I graduated newspapers wouldn't hire a woman, so I ended up being a teacher, and I've struggled financially my whole life, Bug. Don't put yourself through that."

I applied to Georgia and Tennessee but went with Tennessee because Georgia would have cost my parents an extra $1,800 each year. I felt selfish asking for that much money. I should have borrowed it like I later did for graduate school. Then I could have gone to my dream school *and* spring break *and* sit-down restaurants.

I went to UT. I majored in finance. But, twenty-some-odd years later? I write and teach. Money? It comes and goes, but happiness in your work is crucial. The simplest days should be the best days. Why live for the weekends when they represent only 28 percent of your life? Make the 72 percent majority of your time better.

I am following in my mother's footsteps because I am becoming her. She's eccentric, but I hope to top her quirks. She should write books, but she'd rather sit in her chair with a cup of colored pencils beside her so she can daydream via her adult coloring books. Sometimes she makes Christmas wreaths. These days, she's on a homemade Christmas ornament kick. Tall Child got a popcorn-themed Styrofoam wonder while my neon prize was dotted with embroidered llama patches. Sometimes she drinks vodka and diet cranberry juice in a chair down by the river or riding shotgun on an ATV with BBJ as they bump and bounce through their respective Crippled Beagle and Naked Lady Farms. I suppose Delicious is more story *teller* than *writer*. Once my arthritis sets in for good, I'll be more teller than writer too.

This Theory first came to me at my mother-in-law Bop's house in Nashville. It was Christmas time, the MOST stressful time of year when men should do as they are told but instead walk around with knife and fork in hand. Oh, and money you don't have hemorrhages from every gap in your purse, clothes, car, and home. Bop has a small U-shaped kitchen in her Cape Code style, perfectly-sized-for-retiree house. She loves to host gatherings and always employs her poised daughter (Tall Child's younger sister) Dogwood Debutante in her entertaining endeavors. I guess that since I'm female and Southern, I'm *supposed* to help slice ham, pour water into Waterford, and set heavy silver onto polished wood. Boring. I don't sort silverware. I took the enneagram test and my personality style description stated that I feel "mundane tasks are beneath my sensibilities." Yes! An academic excuse! Anyway, Tall Child and I sat in the living room that December day and he coached me to "go in the kitchen and help Bop."

I said, "I'm not sure there's room in there for me." Instead, I poured a glass of wine, perched on the back of a club chair, and observed a mother-daughter kitchen dance choreographed through years of practice. Bop and Dogwood Deb worked like two ballerinas in a music box. They somehow circled, scooted, and slid around each other without dropping a single teaspoon or sloshing hot butter beans over the edge of a footed serving bowl. There was no need for my Pigeon Forge, Tennessee, bumper boat behind to enter the dance. They were not just partners. No, they were one being, and I was *being* out of the way. Christmas means high-stakes entertaining. Had I tried to "help," I could have jacked up the smooth, synchronized sequence. I would have been the primary colored Happy Meal toy whose angles were all wrong, whose lack of grace would have wedged between gliding pastel twirling aprons. Why, I might have capsized the gravy boat or worse, spilled my wine!

I wondered how they could be such a dynamic duo in that kitchen and then realized that Dogwood Deb is becoming Bop. I pondered, *Am I becoming Delicious? Naaah.* I asked Sharky as he rode shotgun on the way to school one day soon after that, "How am I like Grandmama?"

He said, "*Dra. Ma.*" He's referring to the way in which Delicious and I take normal situations and make them urgent, frightening, and stressful. Right now, I am in the midst of a battle with asbestos tile that I chopped up in my basement, a huge dead poplar that looms over my bedroom, and my ongoing love-hate relationships with wine, Marie's Ultimate blue cheese dressing, and three-minute microwave mug chocolate cakes. As I write this, I'm on day seven of Dry January. Observations: Sounder sleep, clearer thinking, boring evenings. Cousin Fuzz calls the family tendency toward drama the "Delicious and BBJ Effect." Think Doppler. Read this as quickly as you can for the best experience.

The Doppler effect can be described as the effect produced by a moving source of waves in which there is an apparent upward shift in frequency for observers toward whom the source is approaching and an apparent downward shift in frequency for observers from whom the source is receding. It is important to note that the effect does not result because of an <u>actual</u> change in the frequency of the source. Using the example [of a bug kicking its legs in water], the bug is still producing disturbances at a rate of two disturbances per second; it just appears to the observer whom the bug is approaching that the disturbances are being produced at a frequency greater than two disturbances/second. The effect is only observed because the distance between observer B and the bug is decreasing and the distance between observer A and the bug is increasing.

If you think I wrote that, I am honored, but I copied and pasted. I hate citing sources. Don't we all? What good are the World Wide Web and Microsoft Word if we still have draft those aggravating works cited pages? I prefer to copy and paste URLs. I found that explanation in one of everybody's *favorite* hangouts, you're gonna want to write this down, www.physicsclassroom.com.

In laymen's terms, basically, when Bug asks/does/proposes anything, The Delicious and BBJ/Doppler-like Effect creates a disturbance in the holler based on paranoia and anxiety. It's a family trait prominent on our East Tennessee compound. For example, I once said, "I think I'll go visit cousin Bags in Florida."

To that statement, Delicious scolded, "Oh, no, you won't. Bug, you'll get raped all the way down there and back."

I was 35 years old.

Delicious and BBJ swing and share apparently big news.

Sharky also said, "You and Grandmama both think you have P.D.H.'s and can diagnose diseases."

I corrected him, so Delicous-ly, "Sharky, you mean Ph. D.'s, and yes, I take pride in my expertise in the prevalence of autism, group dynamics, and the father issues that led women to vote for Bill Clinton and Barack Obama. You just wait. I am on the cusp of a great discovery in clotting disorders." You see, the asbestos tile issue is overwhelming me. I've visited numerous websites in my panicked research, so now the creepy marketing stuff is creeping me out. Every other Facebook post is from a mysterious person warning me of mesothelioma. My chest hurts. I've joined support groups.

Finally, Sharky said, "Oh, and Mama, you and Grandmama are terrible drivers." I do drive with emotion. Delicious punctuates every sentence with her brake pedal, as does BBJ. If anyone close to use is navigating a divorce, it takes us twice as long to drive to Hobby Lobby.

NOT staged: Bug left. Delicious right. See the lines? Look closely for a special greeting.

~~~

My sweet, athletic, sincere friend Wine Box Out lost her mother years ago. She told me, "My mother was my life." I feel the same way. I love and adore and need Delicious to a fault. But, I'm not going to lie. There were things she did when I was growing up that really bugged this Bug and I made silent vows not to repeat. Never heard of a silent vow?

Red Hot Backspace and I attended a marriage class. Yes, together. She's divorced, and did you really think Tall Child would go to a marriage class? I tried. I asked him to go with me, and he said, "No thanks. I hate school and I'm the ideal husband."

I conceded on *one* of those counts and didn't press further. I think that makes **me** the *ideal wife*! Oh well, someone had to stay with Gnome and Sharky, anyway. After my and Red Hot's first class, Tall Child asked, "How was marriage class?"

I answered, "Interesting. Do you want to know all the things you do wrong?"

He said, "Nah. I'm good."

Anyway, in the class, the teacher-preacher said that we should never make silent vows because we are setting parameters that God can and may want to change. We shouldn't limit or fight destiny, right? Are we destined to become our mothers, no matter how we fight? Maybe.

Growing up, I made the following silent vows:

VOW 1: "I will never cut off all my hair just because I'm getting older." Delicious says that once a woman gets a certain age, she needs to cut off all her hair because "long, stringy hair makes women look old and tired."

Then: In high school, I made Delicious late for work because I had to perfect my bangs. You know the drill: One Conair roll up, one Conair roll down, pick, spray. Humidity causes a flop. Cry. Throw a fit. Do over. Delicious bought me highlights and perms. I even got into making Gatlinburg-Pittman High School blue and gold barrettes to sell to classmates. They sold way better than the fish tank "magic rocks" that changed colors. I hustled those all over the Pigeon Forge Elementary School playground. High school girls have money and don't tattle. I was rolling for real.

Now: If I get hot, I get a haircut. If I'm in Alabama, Florida, Nashville, wherever, and I notice my shaggy bangs or what Delicious calls my "dog ears," I get a haircut. I pull over to the first cheapo place like Great Clips or Supercuts. No more tantrums, just $12.00 and some White Rain and I'm content. When I have extra time, I hit Ross and Co. to see my top stylist, California Dreamin'. I chose her to be my top stylist because her son played baseball with Sharky and she's a friend. Bonus: She IS GREAT at her work. Whew! I just tell her, "Cut my hair so I don't have to fix it. I like it wavy and loose, so I can floof it up and not look so old and tired. You know, when you get a certain age you just can't have long stringy hair." What? Who said that?

Recently, Red Hot Backspace's daughter Suspenders enrolled in the local Paul Mitchell school. I set an appointment. If you haven't been to a school salon, go. I love being around students, and the cuts are a bargain, which enables you to tip big. It's a classroom setting, as in rows of salon "desks" where students have all their tools and textbooks in full view. Suspenders fetched me from the front desk and said, "Right this way."

I tried to push her to excellence. When she asked, "What would you like to do?" I answered, "Oh, I don't care. Be creative! Look at me hard, and then do whatever you want. You are the artist!"

She said, "That's terrifying."

"Do it," I said.

The young stylist beside her stared at me and Suspenders said, "Don't worry; I know Bug. She's crazy." Then she said to me, "How about we add some layers? How much do you want to cut off the length?"

I said, "Sure. Layers. Cut off whatever you want to, just make sure I still look like a girl. Leave some hair below my ears."

I felt badly when I said that because her neighboring he/she/him/her/shim/sher stylist's head was completely shaved on both sides with a THREE-INCH RAINBOW MOHAWK from front to back. He had painted black fingernails, mascara, and was obviously nervous. I thought, *I've offended him.*

We'll call him Starlite, after Rainbow Brite's horse. Well, I looked at Starlite and said, "What would *you* do to my hair?"

He said, "I don't know. I'm too busy freaking out to think."

Suspenders chimed in, "He's really nervous"

"Why?" I asked.

Brite said, "I have a perm at 9:30. It's my first one."

"Ever?"

"Ever."

I thought, *If he thinks he's nervous, how does he expect this stranger to feel when she sees Rainbow Brite's horse with a pair of razor-sharp scissors and vat of ammonium thioglycolate waiting for her?"*

He showed me his textbook, which had step-by-step instructions. I wonder if I could cut my own hair *professionally*? I mean, I used to cut my long hair all the time. I just pulled it straight up into a ponytail, twisted it one way, sawed through the rope, then twisted another, sawed through, then showered. FREE! Those books have secrets. I need those secrets.

I coached him, "Okay, well, you are in The 9-1-9, so your client could be demanding. Then again, she could be like me and understand that you are learning."

"Yeah, true."

Suspenders waved her teacher over. She explained what she planned to do to me. He approved.

She got out her school scissors and went to town. At the end, she asked, "Do you want me to cut your bangs?"

I said, "Isn't that customary?"

She said, "I guess so."

I said, "Yes, but don't choke. This is where you can REALLY make somebody mad."

It was fun giving Suspenders a hard time and embarrassing her. I even threatened to yell on my way out, "Well, this is by far the BEST [EXPLETIVE] HAIRCUT I'VE EVER HAD IN MY ENTIRE [EXPLETIVE] LIFE!"

She made a good grade, and I loved my haircut. Starlite's perm lady never showed. Or she did, saw his hair, and ran for the hills. We'll never know.

Red Hot Backspace admits, "I have to try really hard not to wear my hair like my mother's."

Ditto, Red Hot. I'm heading that way. The last time Sharky had a basketball game, I way over-sprayed my hair with Aussie. Just like Delicious. It's a good thing Sharky and I have outgrown our childhood asthma.

VOW 2: "I will keep my house really neat so I can find tape and stamps." Once, my daddy looked at a pile of clean laundry on the floor of our 100-year-old farmhouse and asked, "Delicious, are you EVER going to fold those clothes?"

Delicious answered, "Pooh, are you EVER going to fold those clothes?"

Delicious always told me that housework was the "last thing on her list" and she "had her priorities straight." Yep. Pooh was #1. I was #2. We never had to seek out her attention or energy. My grandmama Buddy lived high on a cedar-stacked hill facing The Crippled Beagle Farm. She told us that often, when Delicious hollered, "Pooooooh/Buuuuug, where are youuuuuuuuuu?" the sweet, longingly bellowed calls floated "over the river and through the woods," up the cow field, and onto Buddy's porch. My daddy and I valued the relief of solitude, but Delicious wanted to be up close because she was interested in every little thing we said or did. Daddy and I hiked all over our 72-acre farm, sometimes at the same time but typically alone. Remarkably, we never crossed paths in those woods and never escaped the doting clutches of Delicious. She may not be a good mopper, but Delicious is a dang fine tracker.

Then: My bedroom, my dorm room, my first apartments, and my first house were always tidy. I took great pride in keeping neat quarters. I knew exactly where my scissors were.

Now: It's been coming for some time. Tall Child and I used to boycott. Feeling overwhelmed by the supposed imbalance of our chore lists, we staged these ridiculous domestic stand-offs where one of us would say, "That's it! I am boycotting for two weeks." The boycotter would do none of his/her chores, so the dirt, laundry, dishes, and to-do's piled into obvious "look who suffers and contributes the most" stacks. I felt a boycott coming on last week, but this time, I channeled my inner Delicious (who is growing stronger by the day) and said nothing. I simply QUIT. Now, I plan to put my priorities in order: #1 Jesus, #2 Tall Child, #3 Sharky and Gnome, #4 friends, ... These days I do as much housework as I feel like doing and slide the rest of the stuff out of the way. Hardwood and my golf course squeegee help.

I hide the tape and stamps, and I buy scissors at Dollar Tree. Lots of scissors.

I took a page from my teaching love Sugar Bear who inspired me with his efficiency. Sugar Bear has a Ph.D. in something I don't understand that has to do with sea oats and weather, and he is a devoted husband and father. I complimented him on his uber-professional junior high work attire one Monday morning. He said, "I always wear a dress shirt and tie on Mondays. Every Sunday when I get home from our worship service, I lay my church clothes out on the chair in my bedroom. This method allows me to sleep another ten minutes on Mondays and save money on laundering."

God first. Laundry second. Amen, Sugar Bear.

VOW 3: "I won't talk to strangers all the time." Most of the time when we went shopping to malls, the expedition was focused on finding "slacks and blouses" for Delicious and BBJ. They loved women's departments. I was miserable, so Delicious bought me a *Sweet Valley High* book as soon as we arrived, and I perched in those club chairs by the tri-fold mirrors to read while she and BBJ tried on one thousand shirts that all looked basically the same, except for the ones with necklaces attached. Those were special.

Then: Those days were rough, but survivable, thanks to Morrison's Cafeteria macaroni, rolls, and Jell-O and the adventures of Jessica and Elizabeth Wakefield. What really stunk was when *I* had to try on blouses and slacks or, heaven forbid, swimsuits. Not only did I have to say, "Don't look, don't look" to Delicious, who came in every dressing room to "protect me from perverts." I also had to endure the critique from sales people. You see, as soon as we walked into the store, some nice clerk would say, "May I help you?" I liked to say, "No, thanks. I'm just browsing," and suffer through swimsuit season in solitude.

Delicious, on the other hand, would say, "YES! My daughter Bug is going to a fancy party with her friends! She needs a dress. Will you help us find one?" Torture for a teenager, worse for a college co-ed. Though the goal was apparel, Delicious ALWAYS found a way to say, "Bug is in the UT band." She was so proud.

Now: *Now* I get it! Delicious wasn't overly friendly; she was BUSY. She was being The Man. I am a working mother of two. I don't have time to browse for a blouse. I'm thinking up a uniform for my workdays. I need something I can wear to exercise, meet a client, tutor a student, and comfortably sit in my writing chair for hours on end. The fabric must not show cat hair. Now, on the seldom days I do shop, I let anyone in the dressing room. And when a clerk greets me, "May I help you?" I say, "Yes, you can! I was in the UT Band and I need a Size 14 . . . ."

A succinct, searing glance from young English teacher Delicious.

1977-78 GPHS 1st 62

Delicious poses once again for a yearbook photo.

What a fierce beauty ready for academic battle. She worked like a man and taught and teaches me constantly about how to navigate humanity, thus I have finally given up and given in to her abundant advice. Instead of fighting the natural current, I now happily hop into the riptide of becoming my mother.

120

I mean, she is always right. In honor of my beloved Delicious, I now whip through Chick-fil-A for a sweet tea with extra, extra ice and lemon and write Sharky's basketball stats and my grocery lists on the back of bank deposit slips. What else are those tiny papers good for?

Theory 31: Old age reveals the true you.

The old saying, "Once a man, twice a child" is at the root of this Theory. Great thinkers from Shakespeare to Sophocles to Plato spun their own unique phrases based on this truth. I agree. Not only do we return to childish ways, but we also reveal our *true* selves. And, yes, our true selves are often replicas of our mothers, but with unique traits we've collected through our individual life experiences.

I watched my precious father-in-law, a gentleman who served as banking commissioner for the state of Tennessee, a philanthropist who led fundraising efforts for an Appalachian community, a husband and father who loved his family with great passion, a "good man" in every sense of the word, become a child in his last years.

It was hard to watch. It was also sweet to see. Why? Because, even though he was frustrated, tired, and sometimes impatient, he became even more tolerant, gentler, and kinder with age. His was a servant leader. That's not always the case.

Some elderly people, especially those who suffer from dementia, get combative. I'm sure there are medical and psychological reasons for this. I am NOT criticizing the sick. When I'm preoccupied, confused, or under mental duress, my family and friends notice. I try to hide my freak parade from my clients. Nothing is more stressful that managing a Roaming Gnome, invoking a high school Sharky to do homework, or working toward a deadline in a creative industry when worried about your marriage, money, a diagnosis, or a hurting friend. The important thing is to own your mood and protect others from it. Delicious had a rough week around the most recent anniversary of Pooh's death and admitted, "I am not fit to be out in public right now. I'll just say something mean to somebody."

Well, Delicious is 72 years old. She is not mean, though she does have a quick wit and could nail some people. She knows things. Luckily, she also has maturity and composure. For now.

When I was a baby Bug, maybe four years old, Delicious, Pooh, and I were at Metcalf Bottoms Picnic Area in the Great Smoky Mountains. Pooh was rock-hopping and fly-fishing his way through the Little River while Delicious and I enjoyed Little Debbie Swiss

Cake Rolls and Coca-Colas as we played at the river's edge. A man walked through our site and chatted with Delicious. He waved his hand and said to me, "Come here. I want to show you something."

I went to his side, where he pointed to a spot on a tree. He said, "Lean really close and look at this snail. He is climbing this tree." The old man and I put our heads together, focused on the tiny creature, and leaned within five inches of the hard-working snail. The man asked, "What do you think about that?"

I replied, "Gross! He smells like onions!"

Think about all the humiliating phrases your toddlers have garbled out. Sharky once asked, loudly, "Mama, where'd that man's teeth go?"

Hands down, Gnome uttered the worst phrase. It was so bad it resulted in a now commonly used Owl Squad hash tag acronym. We took a man-free vacation to Edisto Beach, South Carolina. There were four women and eight children in our rented bungalow. A screened porch stretched across the entire front side of the house, which overlooked an outdoor shower and the ocean. *Naturally,* one of the children got sick. That always happens when mothers try to have fun. *Unfortunately,* my Gnome was our guy. He was still in diapers and maybe three years old, which I guess was a good thing since he came down with the, um, the, um Hershey Squirts.

This was our routine: I'd get him all zinc'd up with the Equate version of Coppertone 45, slide a swim diaper over his soft baby legs, put on his Nemo swim shorts, and carry him out to the beach to laugh and play with his buddies. I would gain a sense of hope via his laughter and my Zing Zang Bloody Mary. Then, as sure as dolphins dip, he'd start. Squirt. Squirt-squirt. Squiiiiiiiiiiiiiiiiiirt. Run, squirt, hide from mama, squirt. I'd then roll out of my low-rider beach chair, stagger/chase him down, and carry him to the outdoor shower. I figured that was better than taking him inside the house. I'd rip off the diaper, hose him down, lather him in Desitin and baby powder, and start the routine all over. On day three, Gnome had had enough. He squirted. I chased. We made our toe-scorching trek to the outdoor shower. Then, as I hosed him off and reached toward him with a handful of Johnson's Bedtime Lavender soap, he screamed, "Don't touch my f#!@*ing butt!"

Reader, I detest the word *butt*.

I said, "Gnome! Hush and let me help you." He cried, I wanted to cry, but above the wooden-walled shower, LAUGHTER erupted. The other Owls and a few owlets were on the porch and had heard Gnome's f-bomb. Now, in group texts, when appropriate (which is pretty often), one of us will end a text with #DTMFB.

All this is to say that I blame his foul language on pain and youth. Old people do have the excuse of pain, but not youth. They should know better. Delicious says, "Age is no excuse to be rude."

That's true, but age sometimes brings about a dull filtering system. In Townsend one day, Delicious and I dropped into a real estate office to visit a friend. We walked in and our friend introduced us to her chubby father (they own the business together). Instead of saying, "Nice to meet you," Delicious said, "Yay! I found the only person in Townsend fatter than I am!"

Geez. I tried to cover, but it was out there. The funny thing is that he just laughed. They are the same age.

We spend years 0-65 building and perfecting our filters through trial and error at home, at work, in sports arenas, at parties with alcohol, and at church when people try to put us on committees. In later years, our friends and family watch those decades of personal improvement disintegrate with one diagnosis or a couple of strong prescriptions.

I tell Sharky and Gnome, "You can think whatever you want. You just can't *say* whatever you *think*. Trust me."

I've read that a child's true personality develops by age seven. Suppose we all follow individual bell curves, child up to man then back down to child again. Does that mean we turn the impetuous 57 and reveal who we are and what we really think?

Also, could you be fighting a natural inclination to lie your whole life? Delicious has become an expert in so many subjects. She also over-shares information, as if the cashier at the convenience store cares why we are in Columbus, Georgia. Somehow, though, she charms everyone. And gets discounts. It happens like this:

Clerk: "Are you ready to pay?"

Delicious: "I sure am! I need to pay for these salted in the shell peanuts because I'm so hungry and I grew up here in Columbus and my sister BBJ are I came home because our daddy is being inducted into the Chattahoochee Valley Sports Hall of Fame. We live in East

Tennessee. My daughter was in The University of Tennessee marching Band."

Clerk: "That's nice."

Delicious: "Yes! We love East Tennessee, but we miss being able to walk on flat ground."

Clerk: "Is it pretty there?" (The fact that the clerk asks a question show Delicious has charmed her.)

Delicious: "It's beautiful."

Such a conversation could last for a long, long time. BBJ is a couple of years younger, so she or I drag Delicious out the door. Thus, my belief is that YES, you become more transparent in old age and reveal the true you. Consider these anecdotes.

A man I knew, a successful farmer and businessman, was always well-behaved; however, when he got old, his doctor's office asked him to use the back door because he talk-shouted offensive remarks at patients sitting around the waiting room. He turned racist. Or did he? Perhaps he was a closet white supremacist all along.

A friend told me that her mother, a woman who spent her childhood in Cajun Louisiana and much of her adult life up North, will say anything. When her India-born allergist said, "You need to get rid of your cat," the mother said, "No. I love my cat. Are you going to get rid of your cow?"

One Christmas, my whole extended family was seated around Delicious's dining room table enjoying chicken salad sandwiches, chili, and chocolate chip cookies when an aunt said, "You know, of all the grandchildren, Property Brother has The. Best. In-laws. Hands down!" My whole extended family of cousins and their spouses were there.

A great-aunt said to Delicious, back in her 80's chubby spell, "Well, Delicious, you have gotten fat. And Bug is well on her way."

In front of a beach crowd of men, women and children, an absent-minded elder in-law said, "Wow, Bug, I never realized how LARGE your breasts are!" I was three months pregnant and wearing a swimsuit. I was already hormonally enlarged and self-conscious. I wore a cover-up the rest of that trip.

For some reason, these geriatric faux pas show up in doctor office waiting rooms. My great aunt Big Chick enjoyed a little revenge in one such situation. A lady across the room looked at Big

Chick and "whispered" to her husband, "Am I as fat as that woman?"

When the nurse called Big Chick to come back to see the doctor, Big Chick walked up to the woman and said, "Hell yes, you're as fat as I am, and a foot shorter too."

Big Chick was my grandmama Buddy's twin sister. One day they drove to Kmart in Buddy's old run-down car and parked beside a fancy vehicle. The man in the vehicle opened his driver's side door and knocked it hard into Buddy's passenger door, where Big Chick sat. Apparently, he didn't notice the two old ladies. My guess is that Buddy and Big Chick were sitting pretty, pretty low in their seats. Well, Big Chick was miffed at his lack of respect for their beat-up car, so as soon as the man entered Kmart, Big Chick opened her door as hard and fast as she could and rammed the man's car door. Multiple times. Then, according to Buddy, they "peeled out" of the Kmart parking lot.

My friend Nan took excellent care of her stepfather until he died at an old age. She's a nurse and explained to me that the elderly often know they are dying and get "visitors." Her Papa did. Papa was a character. At the retirement home, he signed up for every outing offered, like shopping, lunch at Aubrey's restaurant, van rides to the movies, BINGO, you name it, but he typically refused to get on the bus at departure time. He did, however, reign as cornhole champion. Nan went to watch him in the playoffs. He put opponents to shame. As a congratulatory measure, the assisted living home director offered, "Papa, I know you enjoy beer. We have Bud Light and Michelob. Which would you like?"

Proud Papa pronounced, "I'll take the Michelob Light." During one morning visit, Papa told Nan, "I died last night and went to Heaven, but I came back."

Nan said, "Papa, that's amazing. What did you see?"

"Well, I saw your mama and all those women from her Sunday school class. And I saw a tall man in a long white robe. He was bright and had light all around him."

Nan said, "WOW! Papa, you saw Jesus. What did you say?"

"Nothing! I don't *know him*. I got the heck out of there!"

During a lunch with my authors guild, fellow scrivener Mr. Charisma (now well past 80) made a stunning declaration. Handsome Sam brought up the topic of how Hollywood actress are fighting back against sexual harassment. He asked the table, "What do you think about these women getting molested nowadays?"

Mr. Charisma answered, "I can't get in trouble because all the women I molested are dead." Remember that these gentlemen use old timey vocabulary. Definitions of *molest* range from "pester" to "abuse." I assure you that neither of these fine men abused anyone. Pester? Yes. As usual, when a thought or sentence is too good to forget, I immediately write it down.

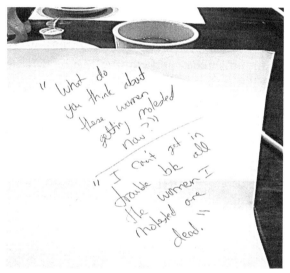

Note the coffee at lunch – another sign of aging.

Tall Child's Aunt Shorty is 85. She's tiny and sweet, like a gray-haired pixie who chirps love and joy, no matter the subject or situation. Well, Shorty has lost some filters. Last year, at a party, someone asked her, "How long were you married?"

Shorty sang, "I was married *55 years* and my husband died. Now it's time to have <u>FUN</u>!"

Theory 32: Teachers are money hustlers with ADHD.

A DHD, for those of you who aren't using your son's Adderall to get through quarterly bank officer meetings, stands for Attention Deficit Hyperactivity Disorder. The *H* is crucial, as it denotes the frantic aspect of the affliction. Tall Child was diagnosed with ADD back in the day. Trust me, there is no *H* in his chart. Otherwise, he'd "finish the drill" (A-Boo's terminology) when it comes to household tasks that he begins and I complete.

I don't see ADHD as a disorder at all. I think it's more a virus we catch via circumstances and excuses. Only two years into my teaching tour, I should have been focused and sane, but, having been surrounded by tenured teachers and middle school students for multiple months, I began to wonder . . . and wander. One of my students asked me, "Mrs. Bug, what medicine do you take?"

"Me? Zoloft, B complex, baby aspirin, and a multi-vitamin."

"No, I mean for your ADHD."

"I don't have that."

(Students laugh in unison.) He said, "Oh, yes, you do."

"Well, if I do, I caught it from you."

~~~

During my planning period, I remarked to Red Hot, "I think I have ACDC."

She asked, "The CD? In your classroom? Huh?"

I said, "No. The disease. I think all teachers have it."

My days were packed with teaching, writing, reflecting my way on paper on weekends to a master's degree, managing my side-hustle publishing company, raising Sharky and Gnome, and helping Tall Child find everything ever. Oh, and I was on that pre-breast reduction anti-snowman-appearing low carb diet, so I was constantly cooking meat. I don't know how the pioneers built log homes and herded cattle without crock pots. Maybe they kept those big cast iron pots over fires for hours and assigned one of the dozen double-named children to keep adding wood underneath the stew.

"Jimmy Wayne, tho' some brush under 'at kettle and stir the nutria gumbo."

What would they think of Campbell's Cream of Mushroom soup? What would they think of crock pot liners?

Okay, see what I mean? I ramble. Once a teacher, always a teacher. Don't all teachers ramble? Don't all teachers stop in the middle of a lesson to tell some irrelevant story? Yes. They earn that ADHD. I'll tell you a secret. Teachers get bored. Imagine 'splaining something for four, 75-minute blocks of eighth grade pre-algebra, five days in a row. How interesting can one make $y = mx + b$? Teachers get bored, so they stop and entertain themselves—hoping students enjoy the breaks and don't tattle. Was it bad that, in the middle of excellent Excel software instruction, I leaned out of my classroom window and yelled at the practicing marching band members, "Play Rocky Top!"? Go band!

Maybe teachers get bored because they aren't motivated. Student motivation is a key component of high-quality instruction. Educators are supposed to motivate students by posting student work to walls and online sites, recognizing and rewarding performance, having one-on-one conversations with each student each day, calling parents, and using imagery, sounds, aromas, and whatever works to arouse student senses to the point they actually *want* to do math or read Shakespeare. Maybe *arouse* isn't the best word. Red Hot burns essential oils in her computer lab. Teachers with "behavioral kids" keep the lights low. The list is insanely endless. But, how are teachers motivated? The list is short.

1. Gratitude
2. Paychecks
3. Uninterrupted lunches and planning periods

We all know teachers are overcommitted and underpaid. It's cliché. Teachers have families and habits to support, so they resort to money hustling. Working two jobs at the same time requires skill, synergy, and smarts. Doing so contributes to the ADHD crisis. For example, I drafted this chapter when I was still teaching. To illustrate, I stopped teaching (sort of) to do field research. I composed the prose as my 35 students worked on their 35 hopefully porn-free virtual labs. Each time I was interrupted, I typed *squirrel*. In 45 minutes, I typed "squirrel" twelve times. Twelve.

Do you know how hard it is to do the teaching thing and side hustle thing at the same time with twelve interruptions in 45 minutes?

In my first year teaching in an urban school, I couldn't pronounce some of the students' names. The school is an English as a second language hub and quite diverse. I nicknamed the boys and girls based on behavior, but in an American Indian fashion. Political correctness is not my strong suit. I'm a humorist, for heaven's sake. I taught a lovely girl who made ugly grades. She never sat down, so I named her Always Stands. One creepy boy said and did nothing in class except read. I called him Sneaks Books. Then, there was the supreme interrupter. This girl had one of those three-syllable names with extra punctuation. It matched her personality. I called her Comma to the Top. Full disclosure: she gave me the priceless pseudonym for the apostrophe. Her material, not mine. She has lots of material.

One day, it dawned on me that fast typists could make some cash tapping out other kids' papers. I suggested it to my prodigy Speed Typer, and Always Stands shouted, "Mrs. D, you a hustler. You always tryin' to make money."

I said, "Of course I am, Always Stands. Remember when my cell phone rang during class? That was a bill collector."

In My Face chimed in, "Them people be callin' my mama too."

Friends, my first year of teaching, I paid $1800 in daycare before I got my first teacher paycheck from Knox County, which was $1900. So, yes, I *had* to hustle. I told my affluent friend OMGG the sum of that first paycheck, and she laughed the mall-bought mascara right off her face.

Here, I toss out only a few adventures in money-making that my teacher friends and relatives have attempted in hopes that young people who read this will take heed. Squirrel! Note the cautionary headings.

Finish your homework for English class. Your teacher may stir your green beans this summer. Teachers know concessions stands, so transitioning from school to restaurant work is natural. Plus, living in a series of tourist towns that lay a path to The Great Smoky Mountains gave my teachers ample hustling opportunities. Delicious, Mooch, BBJ, Moon, Baby, and others tossed salads and dished desserts to nine million tourists gobbling through Pigeon Forge and Gatlinburg. Delicious made appearances at Hobie's, Howard's, The Green Valley Restaurant, and Applewood. I don't know many Gatlinburg teachers who *didn't* serve a tour at The Heidelberg Restaurant at Ober Gatlinburg (where the Tram lands). Even the grammar school music teacher, The Instrumentalist, donned lederhosen and played brass and percussion for the Oompah Pa Band. Gatlinburg-Pittman Highlander teachers quickly shed their winter kilts to make some German summer dough.

Students, don't picture your teachers naked. Once, in the teachers' lounge at Gatlinburg-Pittman, a then chunky Delicious joked, "I am sick of waiting tables. I may try prostitution this summer."

Her co-worker Πr^2 said, "You should charge by the pound."

Don't eat the yellow snow cones if you smarted off in history class. Handsome teacher Magnum P.I. chipped and flavored ice for hot tourists on Gatlinburg's main strip. Our Honors Typing (that's what *we* called it) teacher Goose powdered greasy funnel cakes in his own booth just a few yards away. Synergy.

Late for practice? That may cost you extra at the baseball card show! Magnum P.I. also hosted the occasional baseball card trading show in a borrowed hotel conference. My then twelve-year-old cousin Roscoe and his middle school friends helped P.I. out. Once, Roscoe begged me, "Bug, give me just one of your summer paychecks and I'll double it at the baseball card show this weekend." FYI: Don't have a car wash at the top of a mountain, right Roscoe? Hustle smart.

Students, you may think they're lazy, but teachers get physical in the summer. Mystery Coach loaded—hand-under-hiney style—tourists into sight-seeing helicopters. Enjoy that Sigma Chi chalet party during rush next year, seniors. Your English teacher will be wrapping up her cliff-dwelling cabin housekeeping work and pulling out in her Impala just as you back in to unload your kegs.

Grammarians with gusto make great tour guides. Teacher Tush *owned* the microphone when she hopped on crowded tour buses as they cruised into the Smith Family Theater parking lot in Pigeon Forge. By the way, most Sevier County/Branson City/Atlantic City/Disneyworld/Las Vegas entertainers are teachers who have summers off.

Want extra credit? Bring your married aunt and uncle who make a combined income over $60,000 and have credit scores over 650 to Coach Bama's timeshare booth! Timeshare booths perch at busy spots along tourist drags. Calm, sweet, honest Coach Bama raked in a few good sales pitching annual two-week "ownership" of mountain cabins to targeted tourist audiences.

Students' *parents*: Support your teacher friends when they hustle. They will return the favors when your child has a 69.5 in chemistry. I held a Bug Camp a few summers ago. I toted and hollered at five campers for five days. Sharky, Gnome, Brother, Boyfriend, and Angel #3 picked blackberries, swam, played Monopoly, and cruised The Crippled Beagle and Naked Lady Farms. I scored a little cash and a priceless week with my friends' children. I promoted Brother, who at age twelve was my oldest participant, to camp counselor, which really meant he could sit in the front seat and bruise the other campers when they got out of line. The role served him well. He documented the experience in his college applications and used me as a reference.

Prefer a sanitized inner tube for the lazy river? Get your pronouns straight. Teacher Wild Onion expertly doled out tubes to SPF'd tourists at a local water park. Meanwhile, just across the cement pond, sweet science teacher Daisy served up nachos and fountain drinks.

Practice your clarinet like a good geek because your band director may soon be your boss, or worse, your employee. As a teen worker at The Track, I handed out skee-ball prizes to indecisive goobers. I rescued fat tourists who lacked hand-eye coordination as they frantically circle spun strained rubber boats in the center of bumper boat pools. To this day, I detest the combined smells of gasoline and chlorine. I handed out golf clubs and neon balls in the putt-putt booth. All this time, I labored under the watchful eye of my high school band director, Music Man. Music Man moved up the management ladder quickly. Track owners trusted teachers to separate scraped up tourists from go-cart asphalt and serve concessions. Teachers are used to saying, "Wash your hands," "Wait your turn," and "Do the math"

Mini-Theory: People Can't Count Once They Leave Home.

Teachers who applied knowingly and bravely took the risk of being managed by their own students.

Don't underestimate your teachers. They are trained researchers and industrious risk-takers. Delicious and I made a gamble once. We bet on Mother Nature's bounty on The Crippled Beagle Farm. We heard that one of my elementary teachers was digging and selling ginseng for over $1,000 a dried pound. We freaked because $1,000 is serious money. Delicious and I were gonna dig out of the recession with some Crippled Beagle gold!

We made a plan. I scoured the internet and learned to locate ginseng using companion plants, to dig only plants with three or more prongs, and to pull the plants that had at least five years of maturity. I knew how to dry and sell the roots and even lined up two buyers. I watched videos and printed pictures. We set a digging date. Obviously, plants are easier to find in the spring, but we were fired up, so we started our hunt on a cold, wet, January Saturday. We wore old farm clothes and carried shovels and grocery sacks. Delicious did no research, so the moment I told her ginseng grows on steep hills, she choose to support me from below.

Delicious poked her walking stick through mud and black walnuts behind the barn and made a verbal shopping list while I climbed, slid, and cussed. My miserable hunt lasted 90 minutes and resulted in three plants. With my misted hair, aching knees, and desperation for easy money, I saw mirages in the undergrowth. I dug some kind of ginseng fool's gold. I may try that again some spring, but I'll certainly stay on my farm. I heard a rumor that our teacher friend was arrested for poaching in the Great Smoky Mountains

National Park. Do you know how much dried ginseng it would take to post bail?

Thar's gold in them thar hills!

The ultimate teacher hustle is SUMMER CAMP. Every student must attend a summer camp run by a teacher. This is a hidden rule in school day society and non-negotiable if you want favorable treatment the following school year. Plus, you get T-shirts. Consider these fantastic options to build muscle and brown-nose:

Basketball camp
Basketball *fundamentals* camp
Football camp
Football *fundamentals* camp
Quarterback camp
Baseball clinics (The use of the term "clinics" allows teachers to charge more. Fancy words = fancy prices.)
Tennis clinics
Golf clinics
Track, swimming, soccer, and so on.

For the non-athletes, we have:

Robotics camp. I have no idea what that robotics are, but they are everywhere.
Art camp. Pay to color.
Music camp. Pay to practice.
Dance camp. Pay to twerk.
Invention Camp. Now, if Gnome invents something good, I could actually make a return on my investment. Hmmm. Who owns the rights/patents to these inventions? I think I just figured out who is the smartest teacher-hustler.

Shameless plug: I will be teaching a creative writing camp at The University of Tennessee this summer. Be warned and sign up. Mama needs a new pair of flip-flops.

Teacher hustlers, do the math:

20 students x $100 tuition = $2,000

$1340 for a two-bedroom condo at Edgewater Resort in Panama City Beach for six nights in July
$100 cleaning fee
$560 for gas, groceries, and meals

Camp Session II will pay for your liquor and souvenirs. Yeah, you plan to do the whole "We'll just save money by eating sandwiches in the room" thing, but three Salty Dogs later a teacher-hustler needs some fried shrimp and batting cages.

Double-hustle ideas I've seen:
- Snack wagons - Committed, pro hustlers know to invest in discount store memberships. A 30-pack of varietal potato chips costs around $30. Teacher hustlers can charge $1.50/bag, netting $15. $15 = two margaritas or one margarita *and* nachos at Pineapple Willie's.

- Campers get thirsty. A 24-pack of Powerade drinks costs $12.48. Parched roboticizers(?) will pay $2 for blue liquid refreshment. My guess is that robotics kids like neon beverages. Profit: $35. A teacher hustler can get a solid beach buzz with that margin.

- Keep overhead low. Wise hustlers use school grounds and equipment. They hire student-workers who need service hours.

You may be asking, "How do teachers work all this out as they inspire and educate 35 students per hour, five hours per week?" Planning periods. Delicious knows a mediocre educator who runs a cat rescue business out of her middle school classroom. One of my former teaching colleagues said just last week, "I think I've designed an app that I can retire on." Well, if that doesn't work, there's always the multi-level marketing shop in the teachers' lounge.

Theory 33: Dang you, Tupperware ladies, dang you (but I do love your products).

Downtown Queen P told me, "I was so happy when I retired from teaching so I didn't have to buy any more junk from my colleagues! If other teachers are so broke they must sell stuff to cash flow month to month, what makes them think their teacher friends can afford to buy said stuff? Every time I went in the teacher's lounge there was some product or some catalog laid out by the microwave."

Whenever I am lonely and broke, providence intervenes. I get an Evite or a group text for a fun girls night out. I think, *Ahh, just what I need.* Then I read the subtext: "We'll enjoy snacks and beverages as we peruse new items from my friend [name's] spring collection of [name anything made of cloth, beads, ceramic, or resin]. As I write this, I have two hanging invitations: Cabi and Noonday Jewelry. The ladies are wonderful, and I'd love to spend time with them, but how do I do that without making a $78 purchase? Sharky is on a Zaxby's bender and Gnome's basketball fees are due soon.

Here is a related quote from Wikipedia. Yes, boys and girls, I am quoting from Wikipedia. I don't have time to find a journal article, identify evidence in the text, and use MLA citation to credit the source. I'm busy hustling. Anyhoo, here's what some unnamed but totally accurate contributor says: "Tupperware pioneered the direct marketing strategy [and made it famous with] the Tupperware Party."

The very term *Tupperware Party* is an oxymoron. I think I'll host a fun girls night out and call it Folding Clothes Fun." BYOBasket. What's entertaining in a lesson on salad containers? Then again, who doesn't love a dish that can fly but not shatter?

Thanks so much, you direct marketing pioneers. Yes, you've liberated some housewives but also forced them to sell and shop by capitalizing on the trifecta of issues women constantly struggle to balance: being good mothers, shopping, and guilt. And, you Jack Daniels up the scene, which seems unfair and likely illegal. I mean, do y'all really think the nail salon with, um, chain migration technicians, actually has a legal liquor license for that wine up front? And, what if we let the buzzed public browse Walmart? Delicious's layaway account would set new records! I totally understand the three components of what I call the Tupperware Trifecta. I'm not sure if that makes sense, but I'm been real into the word *trifecta* lately.

1. Time for Family

Women want more time with their children. When mothers work, they wonder and worry. Every time Gnome goes to the school clinic, the nurse calls me. Every time I see that number, I freak out. He goes to the clinic a lot because he likes attention, not because he's sick or injured. Sometimes, his cuts are so small no adult can actually identify them. It is not physically possible to survive three black widow bites from webs in the gaga pit in one week. Women need time with their children, even though that time isn't necessarily easy or entertaining, just like children need time with their mothers. It's unnatural to be apart for ten hours, and I HATED being 45 minutes away from my sons every day when I tried miserably to sell annuities to farmers.

2. Shopping

We are gatherers and talkers. We need other people. Tall Child thinks he shops sometimes, but he doesn't. He thinks buying groceries means buying food. He's clueless. If he turns hero on me and buys groceries on a Sunday we run out of all paper products by Tuesday.

"Tall Child, did you really go to the grocery store?"

"Yes. Didn't you see all that cheese?"

"Yes, but we are out of paper towels, aluminum foil, soap, cat litter, detergent, diapers, ..."

"Oh. Okay. I'll hit the DG [Dollar General] during my lunch break."

Women must gather lots of things and say lots of words. It's who we are. So, the Tupperware Trifecta addresses our natural instincts to procure and pronounce.

138

3. Guilt

Most American women work. I don't know the stats in other countries because I don't have a passport. When I was a housewife for the blink of a bloodshot eye, I felt guilty for not helping Tall Child pay bills. I concocted schemes like selling flowers out of my yard, being a substitute teacher, and eBaying my way to the beach and back. In case you want to make some easy cash, know that large ladies' swimsuits and size ten dress shoes are huge sellers.

Mini-Theory: All transvestites are over six feet tall and live on rural routes.

I got more and more ambitious. Tall Child complained that his then employer, a real estate developer who owned hundreds of condos, fired the cleaning service because the housekeepers were constant no-shows. I asked, "How much do you pay them?"
Tall Child said, "$100 bucks a unit."
I made a proposition. If Tall Child's company would pay me every Friday, and I could do the work only while Sharky was at kindergarten (7:45 a.m. to 1:30 p.m.), I would clean the condos. They hired me. Of course, my inner hustler got excited. I created a logo and named my business Rental-Ready Cleaning Company. I rode my broom one sunny morning to meet Tall Child on my first assignment. He let me in, showed me the unit, and said goodbye. He forgot to inform me that the condo had no water. I used countless rolls of paper towels, store brand window cleaner, and 409 to scour drywall bits and dust off every surface. My vacuum sucked up all kinds of particles, so much so that my own home smelled like new construction every time I vacuumed. The BEST parts of that job? No boss, no coworkers, no employees. Well, except for Braided Hammer. He was the "finisher" who would wrap up small jobs to make the build complete. He wore jeans, a long braid, and bathed in nicotine and ethanol. But, I liked him because he had a huge square speaker thing that blasted music. The music was so loud that we could both sing but not hear each other, so it was like we were still working in glorious solitude.
You know, sometimes a moment happens when you just know that stuff is funny, and you stop and laugh. I was mopping some

newly laid linoleum as he installed blinds. In different rooms, we belted out Bob Seger's "On the Road Again." Now that's some good moppin' music. I suppose I could have peddled earrings or dishware, but I think I needed something dirty. I learned a lot from Braided Hammer. We chatted over bag/cooler lunch one day.

He asked, "Yer kinda preppy for a maid. How'd you end up doing this?

I said, "Well, I quit a great bank job thinking we'd be okay. Then the recession hit us hard."

He said, "Yep. I bet all 'em businessmen wishes they was plumbers 'bout now."

While men's egos are often, admit it, wrapped up in the work they do, women are more concerned about how their work serves others.

This Trifecta of female characteristics has made Tupperware a legendary household name and made millions of dollars for the countless companies and not-direct-marketing consultants who followed suit. By the way, my friends have sold this stuff, and I wish I could afford to buy more of it. Why? Okay, it's not like the whole supply-demand puppy mill saga. These people are reputable breeders, not sleazy storefronts. Their products are high-quality, aesthetically pleasing, functional, and durable. I want to support my girlfriends' independence, I want them to have more time for people, and I feel awful when I can order only the cheapest item in the catalog. One day my proverbial ship will come in via lottery or a bestseller.

Personal Mini-Theory: I should buy lottery tickets and write better books.

Anyway, when my ship does come in, I plan to say YES to every Evite and buy whatever wins the hostess a trip or next level prize. I also plan to reverse my preferences on Amazon.com and VRBO to sort high to low.

Delicious and I talked one day about how teenagers go gothic to be different but then find themselves in 100-person packs of black-clad, silver-studded gothness. They conform to *non*-conformity, kind of like all those individualistic mountain men in Asheville, North Carolina, who shed their identically groomed facial hair on the hot bar at Whole Foods. I particularly like the conforming to non-conformity explanations we women give when we pick up the direct marketing banner. Here are a few I've heard. Or maybe said:

I've had a revelation.
I really wanted to contribute to the financial security of my family.
This product has changed my life.
I love the products and get a huge discount.
I enjoy spending time with my friends and talking about [brand].
The Lord called me to sell _____. (I want to hear this one this from the intimate apparel saleslady).

Honesty is refreshing and a good sales strategy. Maybe "direct" saleswomen should be just that, direct. They could say:

I am tired of hearing my husband gripe about the grocery bill. I need my own cash.
I want Dollywood Gold passes. Every year.
I miss working, but I don't want to get up at 6:00 a.m. and put on panty hose and have a boss.
I want any reason to hang out with my buddies, drink wine, and shop.
Simple math. If twelve women come to my house, one man will leave.
I'm saving up for a divorce.

I polled my Facebook friends for fodder. Answers were all over the place. I prompted, "Just wondering what you all think about direct marketing and may want to share as I revise my chapter 'Dang you, Tupperware ladies, dang you (but I do love your products).' Who's got the guts to stir it up? Pun intended. Not really. Just happened naturally." I think we handled the whole online conversation with civility. Enjoy:

- *The whole business plan is built on guilt, and I have a very strong case of the Catholic guilt, yet I am not Catholic, so I can't go relieve my guilt in the Confessional. This forces me to buy things to relieve guilt.*

- *I can proudly say I've only been sucked into that vortex once and it was 44 years ago.*
- *I always wonder if the product is so amazing, why isn't it available at Target?*

There is a market for this stuff.

- *I like the personal touch of it and I hate shopping.*
- *The day y'all hear my blood-curdling screams in Glen Cove from down here in "Red Holler" is the day that I will have dropped and broken my perfectly black and seasoned stoneware cookie sheet.*

Competition and brand loyalty don't skip this industry:

- *For the record - I hate LuLaRoe because of the fabricated scarcity of items and inconsistent quality. Weekenders would tell you what you could get instead of having you hope to find some unicorn item that may not exist.*
- *What do Rodan and Fields think of Arbonne, and vice versa?*

Perhaps this is a logical approach, and we are just broke guilty grouches.

- *The products I share with people would be cost prohibitive if they were on a store shelf with the additional costs associated with transportation, storage, advertising, etc. Word of mouth and social media eliminate all those costs, and the money goes into developing and producing the BEST product. The company rewards folks who share the products with cash, which for some, is life-changing.*
- *I'm gonna sell happiness. Oh wait? You have to work for that. Can't pay for it.*

Did I mention WineShop At Home? This is perplexing.

- *Are there any direct marketing, non-pyramid businesses out there? Have to think about that!*

- *So, I see a post from this sales lady . . . with three other ladies in matching navy outfits. I think, well isn't that funny? They wore the same outfit from Cato. Come to find out they were wearing Mary Kay Executive Business suits! Each year, Mary Kay produces a new one, and it is about $400!*

Reader, Mary Kay almost trumps Tupperware. The company ranks right behind Coca-Cola in brand recognition. MK knows how to make money on multiple levels. Perhaps I should apply their methods to my business, Crippled Beagle Publishing.

I could talk women into writing articles for whomever they like and giving me a cut of their fees. They can buy the annual, overpriced Crippled Beagle Publishing standard uniform: Faded Glory yoga pants that tell too much, a tank top to release hot flashes, and the required accessories: Walmart $2.88 silver hoop earrings and a vodka tonic.

Okay, all that was good stuff, but when my sweet friend wrote the following, I felt like dog dumplings:

> *I'm with a fair trade certified company that sells handmade jewelry, scarves, purses and home decor made by artisan groups in fifteen countries, including the US. We use a direct sell model. Each group serves a purpose and helps people who are outcasts or have no hope. Haiti focuses on single parents so they can afford to keep their kids. The one in Cambodia focuses on survivors of acid attacks. Our group in the US helps women escape sex slavery and rehabilitates them. We are about freeing women from stigmas and poverty all over the world. Just because a company uses a direct selling format doesn't make it bad.*

Let's call the super guilt component Guilt Cubed (G^3).
1. I go to the party out of guilt because I'm afraid no one else will.
2. I buy something because I don't want the hostess to fail or everyone there to think I'm a cheese and cracker mooch.
3. I feel guilty at home because I don't need (and likely can't afford) a $300 face polisher when the utility company keeps putting hot pink do not disturb signs on my front doorknob.

I do think women can find success in these businesses, but many need formal education. Before it fired me, the bank spent THOUSANDS of dollars training me to be a professional, efficient, productive sales rep. Here's a quick tutorial for all you living room/teachers' lounge hustlers.

Time the events correctly. Old people get their Social Security checks the first and third days of the month. Set up a booth outside any bank branch between 9:00 a.m. and 11:00 a.m. You can give them coffee and donuts before the banks open because they are all waiting in the parking lot. Teachers are paid monthly. Figure out what day and set up in the teachers' lounges that exact day. Don't come the next day. All their money will be gone. Don't believe me? Visit a teacher breakroom on pay day and watch stacks of bills get paid. Delicious says, "I just don't feel right until I'm almost broke."

Once, I asked her, "Do you *ever* balance your checkbook?"

She said, "No. I like living on the edge."

Remember, teachers are hustlers, but you can outhustle them. Get 'em on pay day, but also when they're tired and hungry, like second period.

Market your products appropriately. A work buddy told me that his Sunday school classmates were telling praise and prayer requests when a fellow Christian said, "I'd like to give praise to my four-year-old son for bringing me my morning Nugenix Ultimate Testosterone tablets." Not cool. Can I get an amen?

Study your audience. Invite people who have money. Teachers, stop trying to sell to other teachers. Spend your summers hoofing it through medical complexes where women are trapped in gray-walled coughing chambers and are happy to welcome food, jewelry, and home decor diversions. Go where your audience is already gathered.

If you rep a product and profess its miraculous qualities, you must exhibit these qualities. My old boss *Bob* repped AdvoCare. He carried a big briefcase full of potions and pills. He told me I needed gingko biloba. Whatever. Anyway, he was not balanced. He cursed at work. His belt is cinched so tightly it's above his britches. He says, "Quite frankly" every other sentence. And, that stuff didn't make him one single inch taller. Someone in my branch bought from him, and that caused a stink. My old (and I mean OLD) teller came back from family medical leave after breaking her hip (yep) and was age-appropriately paranoid about her job. Banks can't discriminate, but I'm telling y'all, she had dementia. Am I a doctor? No. Did she know her email address? NO. Her email address was [name]@[bank].com. Anyway, she found a two-ounce bottle of AdvoCare juice in her money drawer and freaked. She said, "Someone is framing me for drinking on the job!"

Pet peeve warning! Don't recruit pyramid people at your first party. Sell YOURSELF, sell the product, but don't sell the opportunity to sell. That moment you say, "Here's the catalog. On the last page, let me know when you'd like to become a consultant," you lose credibility. Tall Child doesn't sell a truck load of hardwood flooring to a builder and then ask, "If you'd like to be a flooring sales rep, fill out this form." Sell your stuff and you. Your obstetrician is not going to quit being a doctor to rep a children's clothing line. When you recruit coworkers (who should be competition, right?) at the same time you sell products, you're building pyramids faster than Egyptian slaves high on AdvoCare Spark.

For the guilt-ridden invitees, I've come up with a handy list of phrases you can use to conquer G^3 and regret Evites. Hey, it's direct marketing, so stick with the theme. I've tested most of these excuses:

You are serving alcohol and I'm only three weeks out of rehab.

My boobs are too big for those blouses.

I'm agoraphobic.

I don't cook and I never will.

I have edema. Can't wear boots.

I'm not smart enough to figure out how to complete your order form.

My husband is a tightwad.

I'm a tightwad.

[Child's name] has unicycle practice.

My mother-in-law buys all my children's clothes.

I refuse to drink and drive, and can't tolerate the party without alcohol, so, I'm out.

I'm allergic to latex.

You sales-friends take too long to deposit my checks. Boing! Boing!

I too am saving up for a divorce.

~~~

I find it ironic that the "non" multi-level direct marketing company Thirty-One bases its business philosophy on Proverbs 31. If you read the entire chapter, you'll be exhausted. The wife "of noble character" makes clothes, sells clothes, buys clothes, clothes her entire family, and clothes herself in "fine linen." She also clothes her bed. Oh, and she brings food from afar. She buys a field and plants a vineyard. She takes care of the poor. She does NOT "eat the bread of idleness." Well, women over 40 can't eat bread anyway. The Proverbs 31 lady works without rest for 21 straight verses, but my favorite verse is, "Her husband is respected at the city gate, where he takes his seat among the elders of the land." He's shooting the breeze. He can because she's got a booth down the street hustling all the stuff she made on the loom she probably built after she planted the forest that grew the trees that became the wood that made the loom where she sat and threaded the fabric from the critters she shaved after raising them and feeding them with food she grew. BY ALL MEANS, she should then recruit other women to sell said clothing. Another favorite verse of mine reads, "Anyone who does not provide for their relatives, and especially for their own household, has denied the faith and is worse than an unbeliever." (1 Timothy 5:8 NIV)

Dude needs to get up from the gate and help his noble wife pick grapes. Maybe if HE hustled a little harder, she wouldn't have to teach algebra *and* manage a gift shop in the teacher workroom.

Why don't men host these parties? Do they *ever* feel guilty? Couldn't they enjoy refreshments and watch a friend do a grill set demonstration? Maybe they could cook nachos in rubber dishes and try on different designs of belts. Aunt Terrific says it's because they have sense enough to know it's rude to invite someone to a party then ask him to buy something. Cousin Squirrelly Girly says that when men need a tool, they go immediately to Lowe's and buy it in every size. They aren't going to wait for Bob's Manly Tool party scheduled for next week to order something that will show up the next month. What would men sell, anyway? My friends say:

Beer
Car care products
Recliners
Lawn mower cupholders and accessories
Porn

One day, when (not if) the zombie apocalypse finally happens, I'm sure I'll feel awful about this chapter but be glad I bought that Pampered Chef pizza cutter. Bring it.

Theory 34: Never say, "At least you have summers off" to a teacher.

As I write this chapter, my former junior high colleagues are beginning their first day back to school. It is July 24. Sunday night dread has passed, and at this precise moment, 9:03 a.m., middle-aged bottoms are balancing uncomfortably on tiny lunchroom table stools. Oh, and they are looking around. They are identifying the usual nemeses who will hog the copier and ask them to cover classes. They are checking out whose back-to-school diets actually worked, and who has, as Delicious calls it, been *raptured up* and is mysteriously no longer employed at the school. Especially, the women are complaining. It's no mystery that women love to complain. We are detail-oriented critical thinkers. Plus, we are the critical do-ers, so grant us our soap boxes from which we *must* speak because as soon as we step off those soap boxes, we have to dust them. Among women, I believe teachers are the best of the best when it comes to griping. Maybe I could hustle up a "How to keep your employees from griping" in-service breakout session. I can smell the green $$$!

I cannot tell you how many times in my last year of teaching, as I collapsed after a one-hour school-daycare-errands-home commute, I said, "I am absolutely worn slap out" only to hear Tall Child say, "Well, you're about to have three months off."

Really, Tall Child? What kind of new math were you doing there? My last day of school was around May 28. My first day back was around July 24. Now, I never have been able to read a clock face or remember which months have 31 days, but I can promise you teachers don't get three months off. Six weeks. That was it in my district. Sounds eerily like maternity leave…actually, each May, I kind of felt like I had birthed 230 freshmen.

Thus, in honor of all educators out there who must squeeze onion-dipped, beer-battered thighs back into their hellacious short-in-the-stride school attire, I have made a few lists with the help of my social media followers, friends, and former colleagues. Perhaps, teachers, when a moneyed friend from the corporate world or a well-wishing housewife says to you, "At least you have summers off," you can whip this list out and explain to him/her that teachers need summers off to *survive*. But, be compassionate because you may see those silver-liners in a school cafeteria. No matter how hard some people try in the beginning, they still end up teaching school. Trust me.

First, I think it's important that you know *why* teachers are exhausted and need annual, baby-free maternity leave.

What wears a teacher out?

- Doing paperwork for the sake of paperwork when no one reads said paperwork
- Preparing for an evaluation that requires an eight-page lesson plan when the teacher can accomplish the same lesson with a bulleted list scratched out on a Post-It note
- Holding her bladder for eight hours
- Sitting in meetings and learning nonsense cooked up by sales reps, experts, and school board members who have never taught school
- Explaining, using I Do, We Do, You Do, how to carry the one
- Insurance agents in the teacher workroom
- Accepting, deciphering, then rewriting curriculum to match new state standards that follow mandates by government officials who know nothing of education
- Listening to a guy who inherited an oil company tell her how to teach in poor communities
- Continuously counting the number of pieces of paper she prints out of the copier that breaks all the time (I once exceeded my limit by 2,500 sheets)
- Hearing coworkers' personal problems (Red Hot, I apologize)
- Bus duty
- Ballgame duty
- Dance duty
- Club advisory duty
- Any duty before or after school, really

- Long commutes because school districts can't figure out that teachers perform better if they work in the same communities where they live
- Driving teacher cars—if you see a customer swing open her entire car door to get $40 from the ATM or order at Arby's, you can bet she's a teacher
- Proofreading for fellow staff members for free
- Washing two pairs of black slacks every other night
- Helping her own children with schoolwork after teaching school all day

- Frantic phone calls from her own children's schools and daycares in the middle of class
- Returning said phone calls in a panic while breaking up a make-out session or fistfight
- Enduring a personal crisis with an audience
- Conjuring sub plans from thin air, from home, with no internet and a dead cell phone
- Jumping off a colleague's car

- Finding a colleague who can jump off her car (I'm convinced that only rich people have jumper cables)
- Packing pathetic lunches and eating them while surrounded by filth
- Crawling, sitting, landing on nasty floors for a variety of reasons, but mostly to repair equipment necessary to avoid writing a new lesson plan on the fly

Red Hot to the rescue

- Spending $10 of her last $20 til pay day on some student's fundraiser from which the student gets a trip to Europe with her rich housewife mother as a chaperone
- Going to graduate school every other Saturday for five hours and spending $12,000+ via student loans to get a $1,000 raise, which commits her to teach at least thirteen more years to make it worth the expense
- Dieting while surrounded by thin teenage girls who can eat anything and stay slim
- Acronyms like S.A.D, CCSS, NEA, TEA, PARCC, TCAP, TAP, TSSAA, NCLB, DECA, FBLA, EOC, TDOE, TEAM, TIGER, CTE, etc.

- Hosting impromptu 45-minute parent-teacher conferences at Walmart
- Not cursing
- Working in a profession that gets harder, not easier, as she ages
- Sitting in plastic chairs

I call this Room 211 incident "Bambi on Ice."

Remember, most office workers deal with one client or colleague at a time. I mean, let's hope grownups, even groups in boardrooms, take turns. Teachers are totally physically, emotionally, and academically responsible for students' safety, well-being, comprehension, and proficiency as evidenced by output on standardized tests that waste an entire week of school and then disappear on a state transport truck. Corporate person, the next time you have a meeting, imagine grabbing and keeping the room's attention for 60 minutes. Imagine getting your adult audience to put cell phones away. Imagine being responsible for their insulin levels and self-esteem. Now, triple the number of people in the room and have four more meetings just like the first one before 4:00 p.m. Tired? Multiply that day times 180. Tired? Need a few weeks off?

What a teacher does during long summer "breaks":

- Changes lightbulbs at home
- Feeds other people's animals
- Mows the grass
- Coaches
- Refs/umpires games
- Hosts camps
- Sells off her direct marketing inventory
- Writes books
- Rescues tourists from bumper boat and race track spin-outs
- Runs shuttle services for kids of "moms who have to work"
- Does the marine crawl under her front door to avoid baby-sitting other people's children
- Teaches vacation Bible school
- Teaches summer school
- Gets a pap smear, mammogram, dental cleaning, colonoscopy
- Finishes hours upon hours of unscheduled, mandatory, UNPAID in-service training
- Attends professional development conferences where she is forced to room with someone who shouldn't be teaching
- Serves in the National Guard
- Sleeps

What a teacher dreads about the *start* of school:

- Sitting through days of in-service when she really needs to fix up her room and write lesson plans
- Tolerating obnoxious teachers who won't stop talking during said in-service meetings
- Spending her own money on classroom supplies
- Learning new software, again
- No day drinking until Thanksgiving
- Taking a shower every single day
- Conforming to a handbook that has rules inside

- Learning students' names (then learning the same students' names again after Christmas break)
- Saying the same thing one thousand times per hour per day per week per month
- Saying the same thing one thousand times per hour per day per week per month
- Saying the same thing one thousand times per hour per day per week per month
- "Yes, I got a haircut."
- "Yes, I got a haircut."
- "Yes, I got a haircut."
- Hearing bells while hung over from the Sunday night dread overindulgence habit
- Moving classrooms, all that hot glue wasted, and going back to the thrift shop for more decor

Which view is better? Compare and contrast.

All that griping aside, I truly believe that teaching is the most important profession in the world because it impacts every other profession. Think back to the people who inspired you as you grew up. My guess is that if you make a list of the ten people who encouraged and loved you throughout your childhood, half or more of those people are teachers. I have been a corporate worker, a housewife, a teacher, and a writer. I miss teaching, but writers don't cotton to rules. Schools have rules. So, I'm out. For now.

To end on a positive note (since teachers must model appropriate attitudes toward learning for their students), I close with wonderful aspects of the teaching profession. I mean every single word. I miss my teaching buddies, especially Red Hot Backspace. I miss witnessing meaningful interactions between the young and the old.

Go teachers!

Teachers enjoy colorful, dynamic workdays in what I consider a calling, if not a ministry. They are privileged to lead children, many of whom need parenting. Teachers socialize with interesting, colorful, funny coworkers who become a second family. Teachers get to learn all day every day. They play personal roles in real lives. I miss those days and those people. As a writer, I spend most workdays in total isolation, and I work almost every single day. I really miss fall break, Thanksgiving break, Christmas break, spring break, snow days, and summer breaks on a budget.

Theory 35: A great summer can be free. Ask any redneck—like me!

As a former teacher and current writer, I am an expert on FREE fun. One afternoon a few years ago, I pulled Big Red into the gas station at my interstate exit. The spot is a friendly but tiny station where SUVs maneuver like Chinese puzzle pieces. I was there to gas up for a little road trip to the river. As I was about to pull out, I spotted a beautiful scene. A scene that screamed summer. I watched a good old country boy wearing sunglasses on a rubber rope and a late July caramel tan dump twelve cans of Natural Light and ten pounds of ice into the cooler that sat on his open tailgate. He made my day. Was he headed to the lake? The mountains? The in-laws? I thought about asking him to pose, but, again, I had to get out of that parking lot puzzle alive, and I'm not big on the aggravation of media releases, so I snapped a photo from my car window. A couple of weeks ago I spotted a chunky little boy, maybe ten years old, literally DANCING as he waited for an ice cream at Brewster's. Ah, simple summer delights.

Ask any redneck, or teacher, or teacher's child, or country boy, broke college student, or writer, and she will tell you: The perfect summer doesn't cost much if you are smart and imaginative and OUTSIDE. I tossed "redneck" into the mix because I lean that direction during hot months. I'm seasonal. Fall: academic. Christmas: stressed out working mother witch. Spring: Bohemian who craves grass (under her feet). Summer: Redneck. Redneck, by my definition, just means someone who spends lots of time outside, for a living or by choice. Think tan lines, not restaurant behavior or upbringing. Think park rangers, construction workers, road crews, the guys at the Panama City Beach serpentarium who toss raw chicken to alligators, and the mile-high teenagers directing tour-ons down water slides.

Growing up, my summers in Sevier County, Tennessee, were awesome. "Awesome" was a big word in the 80's at Pigeon Forge Elementary. Actually, BBJ, who taught at PFES, got so sick and tired of her children, nieces, and nephews saying "awesome" all the time that she banned it. We needed a replacement word, so cousin A-Boo looked up *awesome* in the thesaurus and we adopted *wondrous*, which soon became just as obnoxious as *awesome*. Anyway, once school was out, we had long, hot, awesome-wonderous summers during which we played hard. Back then, season passes to Silver Dollar City, which is now Dollywood, were affordable. Vacation Bible school was free. My cousins and I swam for nothing at the Chalet Village and Riverside Hotel pools because Pooh and Uncle Gravy worked for the hotels, respectively. We tubed and skipped rocks in the Little River in the Metcalf Bottoms picnic area. Delicious and I watched Pooh fly-fish at Elkmont and Greenbrier in The Great Smoky Mountains. My Barbies threw fabulous parties in Kellum Creek on The Crippled Beagle Farm. And, you haven't had a real summer experience as a child unless you've ridden in the back of a pick-up in Seale, Alabama, to get an ice cream sandwich at a store whose floor is dirtier than the bottoms of your bare feet.

Even folks who work year-round like I do now have background knowledge—imprints from childhood's stress-free summers of simple pleasure that make workdays feel lighter in June, July, and August. Just last night, Tall Child and I took an 8:00 p.m. cruise to Cookout for chocolate milkshakes. He would NEVER do that in

November. I equate summer with certain foods, all of which are cheap. When I work in the yard, I earn myself a cherry Icee. When I must dine out with men or children, I take roadies and drink house wine at the table. When I must eat outside, I take cold roadies and drink cold drinks at the picnic table.

Agape Agave says her Edisto Beach trip (all women and children) tradition is to bring a giant bag of Flavor-Ice pops. I can't rip those things open with my gompers. Flavor-Ice should sell safety scissors with every box.

In this Theory, I describe what I happily remember from childhood and enjoy now as a mother. I polled my social media followers and friends and asked for their favorite summer outings. If one said, "Trip to Greece," I ignored her. If she said, "Trip to see *Grease* at the drive-in on Highway 321," I applauded and included her.

Back in the day . . .

Summer brought cousins from an exotic place called Alabama. These cousins were wonderful equalizers to the usual crew as they inserted new ideas and energy into tired games and routines. You see, Roscoe, GT, Fuzz, and I got tired of each other, but when A-Boo, Bags, and Boone spent June-August house hopping and Spaghettios gobbling under the watchful eyes of BBJ, Delicious, and Buddy, they brought with them original ideas and excitement. And, they were low maintenance. Boone wore baseball cleats to Tennessee. He arrived ready. A-Boo and Sallie carried garbage bags filled with summer clothes and shiny swimsuits. Best of all, they were (still are) smart. We upped our games from Candyland and Connect Four to Scrabble and Trivial Pursuit. We covered math too. Nothing beats a flying Monopoly board on a humid porch at twilight. As in "Bring it on Sevier County School System. We done practiced all summer long!"

The grownups repeatedly told us, "Use your imaginations. Inside or outside. Make a choice and stick with it. If you're in, you're in. Once you're out, you're out."

I rigged my bedroom window screen so that once we were out, we could easily sneak back in to play Chinese checkers.

We used our imaginations well outside. In the cedar forest on The Crippled Beagle Farm, we built elaborate houses using sticks as two-dimensional framework. We outlined beds with field stone and packed the rectangles with moss for cushiony mattresses. Sometimes I had a roommate, but when she started telling me how to decorate my kitchen, I moved out and built on my own place. We served up mud pies from our imaginary restaurants. When housework got old, we tortured animals. We put makeup on my old beagle Charlie and covered him in twist-a-beads and ribbon belts. His hot pink pedicure topped off the look. Pooh called the miserable hound a transvestdog until Charlie eventually rinsed off his dog drag in Kellum Creek. I heard some children poured salt on slugs and tied kite string to June bugs and watched them zoom in circles until they dropped dead. I didn't do that, but I did shoot a bumblebee out of the air with one shot from my Red Rider. A real highlight was watching Uncle Trout kill rattlesnakes with a nine iron. We dipped dogs in five gallon buckets filled with water and tick repellent. Envision a dunking booth filled with sticky water, hair, and bugs. Once dunked and delivered, the dogs violently shook off the green liquid and tore off into the woods. The liquid covered our mosquito-bitten legs. That mess justified yard baths. Yay! We stripped down naked and sprayed each other with the hose pipe and ran around the house to air dry.

Grandmama Buddy supplied us with endless Popsicles from our garden. "Garden?" you ask. Yes. We licked those wooden sticks clean and then planted them in pure manure from the feed store or a relative's barn stall. Or should I say a relative's *animal's* barn stall? We dutifully watered the sticks and, sure enough, the next time we arrived at Buddy's house, she had fresh-picked Popsicles for us.

As we got older, the outdoor free fun became more sophisticated. Our cousins played in South Star Band at the Grand Hotel in Pigeon Forge. They were all teachers hustling through hot months, and we supported them as being audience volunteers. My family always volunteers to get on stage. We also answer questions in Sunday school because we feel sorry for the teachers. Anyway, we children, ages four to fourteen or so, clogged underwater, front of stage, on stage, and to and from the vending machines. Our parents did fully clothed cannonballs and competed in hula hoop contests. There, I learned that having personality makes life better for others and that every performer needs to plant people with personality in his or her audience.

In our teens, the girls read *Seventeen* magazine and sunbathed on my cousins GT's patio in Gatlinburg. We lathered on cooking oil. I tried that on the farm, but my beagles attacked me like a I was a five-foot-four slab of fatback.

Indoor fun consisted of cut-throat board games, playing "store," waitressing, mixing potions *I Dream of Jeannie* style, and arguing through games of slap Jack that typically ended in cousins slapping other cousins.

As an adult, such fun is harder to come by, especially on the dime. It's a good thing I like being dirty and love to eat. Consider my list of ideas for your summer plans:

Find some semblance of a beach within driving distance. BEFORE you go, cook up some boiled peanuts and procure a mix of cold beverages. This usually requires a town-wide scavenger hunt for raw peanuts and an at at-home, hour-long search and subsequent de-mildewing of a good cooler. Boil said peanuts. Don't skimp on the salt because the thirstier you are the cheaper the beer can be. Pack chairs, sunscreen, bug spray, peanuts, cooler, and shoes you can safely wear in water. Old tennis shoes are ideal. Yankees and city slickers always show up at the river in flip-flops. I like to sit on a sandbar anywhere near water and dig little latrines for my peanut hulls while Sharky and Gnome fish and fight.

Annually, Delicious and my boys traipse the Crippled Beagle Farm and adjacent acreage to pick gallons of blackberries. They sweat and scrape through brambles until their fingers are purple and their hands are polka dotted with skin pricks. Then, I lay out the berries on cookie sheets and freeze them. After they are hard, I zip them up in plastic bags so I can taste summer via fattening blackberry cobblers throughout the year. Remember, snakes and bears like blackberries, so keep your eyes open.

Nothing beats a long day of writing followed by yardwork than a chilled glass of pinot grigio as I splash my feet in a plastic pool. Why plastic? It's portable! And, this year, I plan to buy three and use two as raised vegetable garden beds. Tall Child loves when I spend the morning in mulch. He would have been a terrible pioneer. He would have been a pioneer's cousin who wore starched shirts and lived in the big city of Tulsa. I love to get dirty. I also love to get clean in dirty water by soaping up my hair and shaving my legs then dipping into warm orange lake water or cold green river currents with my friends.

My buddies offer other suggestions. Pearl taught her boys to carefully turn over river rocks and grab crawfish. When she was little, she waded through a silty pond near her house to catch tadpoles. I'm sure she let them go on to become frogs. Elaine swatted carpenter bees with her tennis racket. She attended College of Charleston where she stepped on palmetto bugs just to hear them pop. Ah, college fun. Elaine also liked to go bridge-jumping. Just remember, if you can't see the bottom, jump feet first or, as Delicious quotes our country's founders, "When in doubt, don't."

If you are physically lazy, that's okay because summer is a great time to eat junk food. I asked Bags, "What is your favorite thing about summer?"

She said, "Cheez-Its."

Best friend Pearl and I have perfected the grocery store cheeseboard, but our roots are simple. We share a disturbing and waist-widening love of cheese with A-Boo, who lives in England most of the time with Scottish husband Jipper. She misses her simple roots but relishes the cheese shops in the townships around her Bingley home. She remembers where she came from, though, and has taught Jipper to appreciate rural Alabama. He says in his adorable accent, "I want chickens." Sharky has acquired this love of dairy and recently told A-Boo of his passion for sharp cheddar, to which she replied, "Be careful. Sharp cheddar is the gateway cheese."

Pearl and I have created a "lovely" (people with taste say "lovely" a lot) charcuterie (people with taste and money say "charcuterie" a lot too) spread, but East Tennessee teacher-writer style: pepperoni, pickles, grapes, mixed nuts, crackers, and preserves. Jelly is a no-no. The good news is that preserves are on the same shelf as jelly. Creativity is easy with dairy foods and summer. Don't believe me? Here's a summer poem for you. I was inspired by Pooh's love for *The Far Side* and Delicious's recipe, as well as my and Pearl's love of tubing.

At the river, Bug floated in a tube.
To get free, she needed lube.
Her rear has grown wide,
Her tummy won't hide.
But on the river, fat does glide.
Bug desires to be trim,
To someday wear a size slim,
But,
alas,
Her mother made onion dip.
And, nothing goes better with onion dip,
than
Ruffles
Potato chips.
And nothing is quite so hypnotic,
As an ice cold vodka tonic.
And, after a few,
Bug thinks she's thin anyway.

On a gallon of gas, you can find an industrial sprinkler. Stay three
feet from the spigot and enjoy yourself at the county's expense.

Theory 36: Senior superlatives must be modernized and must include teachers.

I got an email from Sharky's school indicating that yearbooks are available for preorder. Yearbooks are old-timey print versions of social media walls. Back in the day, voyeurism was limited to drive-by cruising or yearbook viewing. The ultimate sting was expecting a superlative but losing to an enemy, or worse, a friend. Times have changed. Yearbooks are reference materials while Facebook, Instagram, Snapchat, and the like do the job in real time. Since peeping Tommery, jealousy, and graffiti are modernized, I think senior superlatives should be. And, while we're at it, why not include teachers? The lines are blurred at school and in media. Let's blur them when it comes to labeling and predicting. I'm sounding off because I have a keyboard and energy and memories of high school. Plus, now that I have served a tour teaching in the public school arena, I hold academic hours and street credit. I know of what I speak/write.

Teenagers have always fascinated me. Back at good old Gatlinburg-Pittman High School, faculty, staff, and student body enjoyed mountain ways and school traditions. We held football game pep rallies every Friday during sixth period. Students balanced fat raw potatoes on tablespoons in our comical but truly physical field day each spring. As Delicious used to say, "We try not to let academics interfere with our fun." Seriously, though, we were a standout school, academically speaking. Sarcasm and wordsmithing were as important to the culture as chili cheese Bo-dogs named for our beloved guidance counselor and the Smoke Pit where faculty and students discussed current events and bummed cigarettes from one another. Because our class and town were so small, many of the students were together from kindergarten through twelfth grade. Dating often felt incestuous, from what I heard and did not experience, but heaven forbid anyone date a guy/gal from the redneck rival school that sat in Sevierville, way "below the tunnel" that separated Gatlinburg from the rest of the county. We called the Sevier County High students "tunnel rats." G-P should have hosted an international Scrabble team if such a thing existed. The East

Tennessee mountains are rich in prose, poetry, music, and storytelling. Gatlinburg is an artistic community. Wordy traditions of Gatlinburg-Pittman were encased in the school newspaper, *The Blue and Gold Review*, which was run by none other than our beloved Delicious. Two sections were student favorites: *Cheers and Jeers*—in which students harassed or congratulated each other. "Cheers to Mare for catching a boyfriend," or "Jeers to Mare for steeling TRO's boyfriend." The other favorite was the year-end "Senior Predictions." One brave, sarcastic student wrote a snarky prediction for every other student in the graduating class. Well, that one brave, sarcastic student was yours truly. That was my first experience with a death threat. Of course, someone also had to write a prediction for me. Here you go: *[Bug] will go off to college and room with her mother but die an untimely death when her high school classmates burn her at the stake.* Nowadays, that blurb would make CNN, especially since it was written by a teacher. Ouch. Instead of being perpetually offended, I tipped my scrivener's hat to that witty educator. Students took note and carried the message to my fake grave. There was a funeral scene in the spring chorus show. On center stage sat a tombstone reading, "[Bug] 1974 - 1992. Roast in Peace." I, also on stage, felt duly acknowledged as I squeaked out "Just a Closer Walk with Thee" on my clarinet.

Delicious did not go to college with me at The University of Tennessee, but she did spend the night in the dorm room twice. When I had to stay at Humes Hall alone on Thanksgiving weekend to be ready to board the UT band bus at 5:00 a.m. to head to Nashville to play Vanderbilt, Delicious bunked with me. We ordered the "large student special" from Papa Johns, dropped quarters into the lobby Coke machine, and talked about her UGA days. What made those newspaper predictions so funny is that many came true. Who said, "There is humor in all truth and truth in all humor?" I can't remember, but I love Shakespeare's, "Brevity is the soul of wit." In that vein, I list superlatives that my buddies and I conjured up for modern-day yearbook contemplation.

Modernized Senior Superlatives

Most likely to graduate with a 4.5 GPA and go to community college

Most likely to marry his/her high school sweetheart (same winner of previously listed title)

Most like to go to community college after his parents spend $25,000 a year on a private high school

Most likely to live at home during college

Most likely to take a gap year that that lasts a decade

Biggest dud

Most likely to go to college, dropout, go to community college for three years, then go back to the first college and eventually end up with a Ph.D. at age 30

Most likely to come out of the closet at his liberal arts college (or in the Alabama football locker room)

Most likely to "experiment" at *her* liberal arts college just to appear cool and trendy even though she's in love with an actual male boy

Most likely to walk into a tree while texting

Most likely to reach 1,000,000 Instagram followers

Most likely to marry her coach the summer after senior year

Most likely to cause a divorce

Most likely to go to the county jail for cooking meth in his basement

Wittiest (as opposed to silliest because there is a difference)

Most likely to go to federal prison for embezzling at his father-in-law's company (it all starts in the concession stand)

Most likely to get rich writing HTML and JavaScript, whatever those are

Most likely to own his or her own business

Most likely to indirectly cause the death of rescue workers when he selfishly attempts an extreme sport and must be saved

Most likely to be a bicycle guy and make other people late for work

Most likely to become a philosopher

Featuring Spectacles

Most likely to follow a boy to college and get dumped before midterms

Weakest snowflake

Most likely to marry the only boy she ever dates

Most likely to marry the only girl he ever dates

Most likely to go pro

Go, Gnome, go!

Most likely to win a full athletic scholarship and ruin his sports career with a bad attitude

Most likely to win a full academic scholarship, get pregnant, and drop out

Most likely to homeschool her children

Most likely to become a YouTube sensation

Most likely to come "in like a wrecking ball"

Most likely to have his mother committed

Most likely to own a business that is boycotted for something only twelve people care about in the first place

Most likely to be replaced by artificial intelligence

Worst personality

Most likely to be on her parents' cell phone plan when she's 40

Most likely to commit a white collar crime

Most likely to become an internet troll

Most likely to become a G.O.A.T. in something

Most likely to own goats

Best Twitter handle

Most likely to sell Tupperware, Arbonne, Mary Kay, Pampered Chef, [fill in the blank with an endless list of fabulous product lines]

Most likely to have the ultimate college experience by joining the marching band

Most likely to land on the sex offender list

Most likely to become a teacher even though she hates teachers and school in general

Most obnoxious

Most likely to get breast augmentation

Most likely to get breast reduction

Most likely to morph into the opposite sex but <u>not</u> on purpose

Most likely to morph into the opposite sex <u>on</u> purpose

Latest bloomer

Most likely to own a hovercraft

Most attractive to the opposite gender

Most attractive to the same gender

Most attractive to either gender

Most likely to be stuck up under her mama forever

▲▶ Like mother, like daughter.

1992 yearbook candids don't lie.

Teacher Superlatives

Ready to chaperone

Best dressed

Worst dressed

Most likely to split his pants in a pep rally

Most likely to be fired over a social media post

Most perpetual dieter

Most likely to "borrow" from the Beta Club checking account to pay off a bookie

Most likely to have a contract non-renewed

Most likely to tuck her dress into her pantyhose

Most likely to over celebrate when the weatherman forecasts a big snow

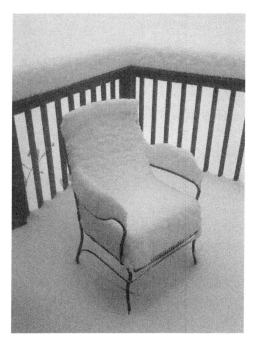

Teacher cocaine

Most likely to marry his student during summer break because he has to make her an honest woman-child

Most likely to sleep in work clothes

Least audible voice

Most likely to drive the same car her entire teaching 34-year teaching career

Most likely to be rude and disengaged at in-service

Least knowledgeable on the subject he teaches

Most likely to get her educational specialist degree and accompanying pay raise and finally leave that jerk

Most likely to show up hung over every Monday morning

Sloppiest desk

Most likely to do all her Christmas shopping in the teacher workroom and from school club/sport fundraisers

Most likely to sniff Sharpies to make it through fourth block

Highest flood britches

Lowest neckline

Most likely to cause hypothermia among students because she's going through menopause

Most likely to think she's in menopause when she's actually pregnant but was too busy to notice the kicking

Most patriotic pervert

Most likely to run out of sick days by Halloween

Hottest temper

Most likely to make love to the principal (once standardized testing is completed)

Most likely to say something in class and then worry about it all night

Most likely to get fired for using her planning period to counsel coworkers going through divorces

Most likely to fist fight a parent

Worst breath

Least hair

Most persistent cough

Most working kitchen appliances in her classroom

Biggest eater in public places

Mostly likely to throw all ungraded papers in the trash

Most likely to hit up a recent graduate on Tinder

Most husbands in a row

I realize that there is no way today's softer, gentler, easily-offended, trophy-choking crowd will go for modernized and teacher-inclusive superlatives. It's sad, really, that we have to be so cautious and so much less funny. I remember the good old days when we could insult each other with fearless flare and laugh at ourselves. Heck, we could even talk aloud about Jesus.

Theory 37: God and prayer are alive and well in public schools.

Did you know that, despite liberal agendas and textbook-rewriters, God and prayer permeate the halls of every public school in America? There's no need for a "Bring Your Bible to School Day" because teachers and many students wear the armor of God by applying psalms and proverbs from bell to bell. If you don't believe me, ask a teacher what he or she whispers under his or her breath. Or maybe don't.

I saw a meme on Facebook during one of the political standoffs that read, "Now that the government is shut down, can we pray in schools?" The picture obviously pokes fun of congressional issues and references the controversial topic of prayer in schools. Back in 1983, my third grade teacher started each day with a Bible story. That was pretty much the only time of day that she had control of our classroom. I remember those mornings and the lessons. She read directly from her King James.

Teachers can't help but communicate ideas that they think students should grasp, including lessons in morality, behavior, and etiquette. A friend of mine once said, "I want to teach in a private Christian school so I can invoke the name of God when I discipline students. Instead of saying, 'You are going to time-out,' I can say, 'You know, God sees what you are doing right now.'"

AMEN! As I so brilliantly (ignorantly) stated in Sunday school once day, "You know, the origin of every story, idea, lesson, whatever, can be found in the Bible." That was almost as smart as the time I told Flower Child, "To me, Easter is the most important holiday," to which she replied, "Yes, Bug. Easter IS the most important holiday." I have lots to learn. Bible reading and church services weren't enough for me. I needed k-12 OUT LOUD education in scripture. Thankfully, my East Tennessee teachers didn't worry about the rules and did sneak in some spiritual warfare.

Think about it this way. What if teachers today could slap a Proverb on every situation? Consider these scenarios.

The desktop publishing teacher has extra ink cartridges and the hungover computer applications teacher's students are wrapping up a huge project, need to print, and have no ink. Should the desktop publishing teacher share her ink with the ill-prepared colleague?

Proverb 2:27-28: *Do not withhold good from those to whom it is due, when it is in your power to act. Do not say to your neighbor, "Come back tomorrow and I'll give it to you"—when you already have it with you.*

The principal assigns two teachers: one male, one female, both married, to design an in-service training for spring semester. They spend planning periods, lunch breaks, and occasional after-school time together and become very close. He complains about his wife. She starts reapplying deodorant mid-day and stops eating string cheese in public. He goes low-carb and drops twenty pounds. She finds out he's tenured and pounces.

Proverb 5: 3-4: *For the lips of the adulterous woman drip honey, and her speech is smoother than oil; but in the end she is bitter as gall, sharp as a double-edged sword.*

Your classroom is out of hand sanitizer. You are dehydrated from over-indulging the night before because you just KNEW the superintendent would call school off for snow. It is flu season.

Proverb 5:15: *Drink water from your own cistern, running water from your own well.*

A student gets caught cheating and is expelled. Students petition the teacher who ratted out the evil-doer. The teacher must respond to them.

Proverb 1:19: *Such are the paths of all who go after ill-gotten gain; it takes away the life of those who get it.*

I really don't know how atheist teachers survive the job. I dealt with the frailties of the human teenage condition on a daily basis. I needed divine intervention whenever I could get it so I could effectively collaborate with all types of personalities, teach disinterested pre-teens and teenagers stuff they never thought they'd need, which, by the way, is ironic because they needed all of it daily in class.

What if I had started my junior high school days with a nice little Bible story? Given the exponential reach of social media and emotionality of national mainstream media, how much time would I have to diet and dye my hair before I appeared on Fox or CNN to defend my actions? I would never want to offend students and parents or cause trouble for my administrators and coworkers, but, shhh, God and prayer are most definitely in schools. Most of us recite the Pledge of Allegiance (". . . under God, indivisible . . .") and then observe a moment of silence. Often, administrators ask students to keep staff members or students in our "thoughts and prayers." I suppose "thoughts" are for the non-believers? I wonder what God thinks of thoughts. I often ask God to interpret my thoughts as prayers because they are far more frequent and far less eloquent. Well, actually, I ask God to interpret my *good* thoughts as prayers. I ask him to forgive my bad thoughts. Sometimes all this thinking is confusing in a school setting where teachers and students must think about their thinking.

Take my first year of teaching. That first year of service should really count for five in the Tennessee retirement plan. The school was rough. Administrators were tough. I'd had enough after one week. It had nothing to do with poverty or race or ethnicity. Those demographics were similar to many American schools, and I enjoyed teaching a diverse student population. No, that school was a special place with fascinating stories, colorful faculty, and an undercurrent, among students, that cannot be explained without bringing in attorneys and school psychologists. In My Face once said to me, "I couldn't be a teacher. I'd hit somebody." Before the early bell rang, I read a devotional, hid my wallet, and, as Job 38:3 instructs, girded up my loins.

Did I want to hit somebody? YES! Did I pray? YES! Every day I read the Serenity Prayer off a little laminated card wedged over my broken gas gauge. That got me from my car to the office. Once "on the inside," I silently repeated an eloquent prayer I wrote for myself: *Dear God, Help me not to cuss, cry, or quit. Amen.*

The perfect perch from which to teach eighth grade pre-algebra

I asked my then colleague Patty-Cakes how he coped and he said, "I just look at a picture of my little girl on the beach and go to the Zen place in my head." He also does Cross Fit. I remember one Saturday when our idiot principal made us WORK. We had to do some stupid accreditation thing. Well, it was a breezy, sunny football Saturday. Patty-Cakes sat in the computer lap gathering evidence of something-or-other and when it was time for the game to start, he announced, with real tears in his eyes, "I should be walking into the stadium right now."

I never cried. I didn't quit. I came really close to cussing, but God saved me with cross-curricular planning. I taught math, which brings out the worst in many people and is a high stakes content area for mandated testing. Frustrated at students' lack of commitment and general academic ability, I blurted out, "How in the hel....k can you not understand this?" My bad. Rookie mistake.

My eighth graders went nuts, saying, "Mrs. D, you just said *hell*," "We're gonna tell the principal and our parents," "Girl, you lost your cool," and "Whoa, Mrs. D, you said a bad word!"

Luckily, I knew that English teachers were using foreign phrases (*alma mater, du jour, e pluribus unum*), so I thought fast and saved my *derrière* by saying, "Oh, no I didn't. *Helk* is a foreign phrase! It's Norwegian for 'I don't know what it is going on right now.'"

They bought it. My error went unnoticed by administrators and parents, but my students employed the word "helk" *ad nauseum* for the rest of the school year. I thanked the Lord.

~~~

Since I know so many teachers, I asked them for examples of prayers they've seen or implemented in school. Teachers can't afford lawsuits, and conservative teachers don't join those "left-wing liberal unions," so I left out their nicknames and paraphrased for ultimate protection.

Heavenly Father,
I'm sorry I let those senior boys get something out of my car and they found Budweiser cans and brought them back into the building.

Don't let my principal find out I cashed a check using the school newspaper money deposit bag as a bank.

Please get [medical office] Anesthesia's financial department to stop calling me at school.

Forgive me for throwing a stack of math workbooks across the room. I didn't hit a student. Amen.

I apologize for wanting to trip that mean eighth grader who called me a "B" and watch her fall headfirst down the stairs.

Get me through the day so I don't say something I'll regret later or that will make me lose my job.

Please get those coaches who pray before games to be that pious during the week.

Thank you for not letting the drug dogs find the dip in my desk drawer.

Please let some disillusioned child call in a bomb threat so we can sit in the sunshine in the football stadium for two hours.

Get that other teacher to shut up so we can end this faculty meeting.

Thank you for not gifting that child hand-eye coordination. If the desk he threw at me had hit me I'd be in some real pain right now.

Please don't let those toga party pictures get out on social media.

It's my day to be observed against a six page rubric of educational performance perfection. I don't want [student] to be sick, but can you make sure it's time for him to have his braces tightened?

Let that tingling feeling be too much Aquanet and not head lice.

Bring precipitation upon this magnificent land you created. Let it snow, let it snow, let it snow!

Parents, you may be wondering, "If teachers are praying such things, what on earth are teenagers thinking during the moment of silence?" I wondered too, so I asked my freshmen. I felt immense shame afterward. I asked them, "What have you recently prayed while at school?" Students gave these responses:

God, help me make good grades.

Jesus, will you please give me the answer to the questions?

Help me treat others like I want to be treated.

May all my answers be right.

Don't let my locker get awkwardly shut so I can't open it.

Allow my school lunch to nourish my body.

Help my teacher forget to check for homework.

Let there be no work in English because I forgot my pen.

I pray for the military and that they are okay.

Keep my cat and my family safe today.

Be with all my friends.

Thanks for providing me an education.

God, lead me down the right path.

Help me through the day. Fifth period biology gets me.

One student shared, "At lunch, we all hold hands and pray. If you steal food during the prayer it's the ultimate sin." Reader, don't be disillusioned by the cynical nature of the teachers' prayers. Be encouraged by the soulful and positive attitudes of today's youth!

Little Greenbrier Schoolhouse: a heavenly setting in which to learn AND pray in the Great Smoky Mountains National Park

Theory 38: Modern education ruined field day.

My son's elementary program equates art, music, and library time with physical education class. What many modern education theorists forget is that physical education, or at least physical play, needs to take place every single day. The business world has figured it out and offers standing desks, treadmill desks, office gyms, and so on. Millennials bounce tennis balls and each other off walls at techy firms like Google and Yahoo. Teachers and students NEED to play outside every single day for at least an hour. Sadly, American public school students often see the hardwoods or dusty kickball fields two or three times a week for fleeting 30-minute stints. Need evidence? Walk any American middle or high school hallway. You'll see way more thunder thighs than we did in the '70s and '80s. Under constant scrutiny, change, and government pressure, teachers and students need stress relief in the forms of sunshine, space, and sports. The demise of physical education and daily recess were precursors to an even bigger sin: the weakening of field day.

I don't know about you, but when nature flips the switch on winter, I feel energized! My feet don't freeze under my writing desk. My car seats are warm. My shrubs and flowers exit a blank, drab dormancy and bloom into the ever-changing technicolor society of my yard. Forsythia shrubs burst with sunshine as Trillium, neon moss, and shiny porch lizards surprise me. Spring also brings nostalgic olfactory-induced anxiety. When I get a whiff of wet grass cuttings, my stomach does a somersault and I have to talk myself down from athletic dread and frustration. Field day looms. Internal conflict arises.

Remember two things. First, I come from a family of athletes. Second, I played sports and sucked at them. Athletic ventures always, always, ALWAYS, put me in a nerve-wracking, self-conscious, embarrassing position (physically and socially). Now at 40+, I don't care much what others think, but as a child, field day was tough on me. It was so tough that it inspired me to write a children's book of the same title. Plus, I am raising two decent athletes. Like any parent, I want to validate my shortcomings by seeing my children overachieve. Field day is my shot! Well, at least it was until modern education ruined it. A little history is necessary.

I attended elementary school during the Reagan administration, when physical fitness was the buzz. My cousins' names decorated the Presidential Fitness Award bulletin board outside our principal's office. President Reagan apparently loved Pigeon Forge Elementary School. I thought we must have been the sit-up, push-up, pull-up studs of Sevier County. Or maybe he gave us lots of awards because he won our mock election with 99 percent of the vote against some democrat. Anyway, while my cousins Roscoe, Nan, and GT anticipated 50-yard dashing their ways to micro-local fame, I personally dreaded the entire experience. Even though I anticipated last place notoriety, I admired athletic prowess and was, as an observer and commentator of human nature, fascinated by the concept and excellent delivery of field day at PFES.

We need to know who the best is. Kids these days would literally pass out by boxed lunch time if they tried field day the old PFES way. For those of you who grew up in, perhaps, softer social settings, let me describe a good old Southern elementary school field day. First, the events stretched over hours, as in bus to bus and bell to bell. School was out. Good times were in. These were our events:

50-yard dash
100-yard dash
400-yard relay
long jump, standing broad jump
sack race
shoe kick, shoe race
potato race
water balloon toss
three-legged race
tug-of-war
crab walk (that one broke GT's arm)
football throw, baseball throw

Teachers organized students a few weeks before field day. Students signed up for the contests they wanted to enter. On field day, teachers escorted students out of their classrooms, down the hallways, and through the lunchroom. In the lunchroom, we picked up uniform lunches that clogged an unusually cool serving line. White bags contained turkey and cheese sandwiches, milk, apples, potato chips, and oatmeal or shortbread cookies. Students carried the lunch bags and blankets and beach towels as well as toys they'd brought from home (children had toys without batteries and screens back then) to the peewee football field between our playground and Frist Baptist Church of Pigeon Forge. Organized by homeroom class, we spread out on the grass surrounding the football field. We traded friendship pins and stickers and talked Cabbage Patch Dolls. Ours was a giant, Appalachian quilt dotted with sticker books, Strawberry Shortcake, Barbie, G.I. Joe, and Scooby-Doo toys.

On the 50-yard line, the principal, PE coach, and judges sat at a heavy wooden table, likely borrowed from the library. Boxes of ribbons waited, heavy with shimmering promise: blue for first place, red for second, white for third. The ribbons came with numeric value and bragging rights. When a student placed, a judge pinned with an actual safety pin the appropriate ribbon to the front of the child's shirt. Well, my cousin Roscoe could fly. By 3:00 p.m. he was a one-boy blue ribbon parade. Everyone in the school participated—students, faculty, staff, administration—everyone. Except parents. Field day was a time of fun and bonding between teachers and students. Parents would be in the way.

Field day was extremely competitive. There was an overall class winner, as in Mrs. BBJ's homeroom. The winning class got to keep a huge trophy for the entire next school year. There was a female winner and a male winner from each grade. And, to make sure everyone knew who was the absolute fastest, most athletic, toughest competitor in the whole school, the judges determined by ribbon count two supreme winners, Mister Tiger and Miss Tiger.

Teachers coached and motivated us to WIN. Winning was the GOAL.

"Oh, no, you didn't say that, Bug!"

Oh, yes, I did.

OMGG wants you to know that back when she was a long-legged Kentucky country girl, she won the long jump. She can't recall the length of her jump, but you can bet the length of her shorts set a record.

Winning was awesome-wonderous! Losing sucked. Even though I was a total goob, I absolutely wanted my class to win. I daydreamed of watching girls I didn't like in other classes cry tears of defeat into their Care Bear sleeping bags. We were innocent, but we were fierce. And, we were physical. No one was fat. Well, no students. And that was normal. Even girls like me who had round bellies and prematurely full training bras could play outside for hours in those days. Soaked in sweat and tap water from burst balloons, our bony shins wore a fur of damp grass clippings. It was heaven for athletes and children who like to be outside. What a concept. Though awkward and nerve-wracking for band nerds with bad coordination and slow-twitch muscle fibers, it was still a social, exciting, book-free, fantastic way to round out a school year with friends and teachers.

Tall Child brought it home back in his day.

Alas, field day has morphed, along with society, to a weaker, politically correct, overall disappointing competitive experience. The 1980's Bug would have loved modern field day as a participant but hated it on a philosophical level. Confused by my love/hate relationship with field day? Think of it this way. I admire success, even when I can't reach it. I admire physically fit women even though I am not physically fit. I just think it's cool when *anyone* does *anything* to perfection. Aren't we all inspired by standouts? You know you tube-sock slide down your hallway after watching ice skaters soar in the Winter Olympics. Admit it. You have tried synchronized swimming at least once, even if you were alone.

Maybe fast-twitch muscle fibers skip a generation. Though I trip in my own living room, can't bowl, bat, catch, dribble, or even swim in a straight line, I produced a remarkable athlete in Sharky. Even more remarkable is that Gnome, whom we adopted, has incredible hand-eye coordination and has been playing golf like a baby pro since he was eighteen months old. The best part of that is that I can BRAG because we technically aren't related by blood, so I'm not technically obnoxious, right? Finally, I am a sports winner! We parents can't help but live and breathe through our children's successes and take on specific, *strong* personalities when our boys and girls show their stuff or when we know they have the stuff but won't show it. Why do coaches make future Major Leaguers bunt? It's just wrong, according to Sharky's grandmothers. If you're wondering what kind of sports mama or daddy you are, check "Theory 10: In youth sports, parents are the real performers."

Several years ago, my field day, I mean *Sharky's* field day in the sun finally came! Or so I thought. You see, Sharky attended the top notch school Gnome attends now. It is chock-full of smart students, thanks to privilege and DNA, who learn under the guidance of superb, tireless, loving teachers. Let's call it Utopia Elementary (UE). The quaint old building is perched a trolley ride's distance from The University of Tennessee and smack in the middle of a wealthy neighborhood (not our neighborhood), so children of professional academia, surgeons, government officials, and downtown ambition abound at UE. At first grade parent orientation, the principal informed us that 92 percent of UE students' parents hold bachelor's degrees and 45 percent hold master's degrees or higher. Wow. I looked at Tall Child and said, "We are running in a fast heat" to which he responded, "Yeah, and bringing down the average."

Well, thanks to our weak DNA and his hearing impairment, Sharky struggled to learn to read. His Kindergarten teacher Veteran invited him to join The Reading Club with a few other boys. Nearing retirement, Veteran rewarded The Reading Club's after-school work with contra-ban cookies and their favorite pastime, reenacting The Battle of the Alamo on the playground. Sharky, a.k.a. Davy Crockett, led The Reading Club against Santa Anna every afternoon. Veteran used play to motivate the reading club and guess what? They are all literate. Sharky loved recess, gym class, basketball, baseball, flag football, and basement ping-pong. He had mad skills too, so after a year-long struggle and true worry about my baby's advancement to first grade, I felt a surge of anticipatory pride in show-off opportunity when I opened his Monday folder to find a flyer reading, *Dear Parents, Utopian Elementary will host field day for all grades on May 14. Please send your child to school in athletic clothing and tennis shoes.*

I high-fived myself and yelled, "YES! Finally *my* baby can do *his* thang! Bring it on, violiners!" The letter requested parent volunteers. I signed up. I have no doubt in my mind that Sharky could have thrown a football or baseball longer than almost every boy in his grade.

BUT, when I arrived at field day, I saw him bouncing on a giant exercise ball with his FEMALE classmate who was his "field day partner." They were singing, "The wheels on the bus go 'round and 'round, round and round, round and round." Really? What. Was. Happening? I thought, *Well, this is surely a dopey warm-up exercise.* I listened for a track pistol, a whistle, or a boombox playing "Eye of the Tiger." From one moment to the next as I strolled through the playground, I bumped into tents of activities and saw no ribbons. Not one time did Sharky get to line up and take off. Sharky's competition for the whole field day was the one girl. GIRL! I was furious. To top it off, they were unevenly matched. She had at least twenty pounds on him. Sharky and his partner (ugh) rotated through stations and got Dollar Tree participation prizes. Prizes? How about ribbons? Lots of plastic, but no glory. I was the only person on the playground who was sweating. I later found out Sharky was doing yoga in P.E. class. Dodgeball is out. Boy splits are in.

I love Sharky's school, which is led by an excellent faculty and is often nationally recognized for being an outstanding public school, but there are many types of human intelligence. At the end of the year, when the principal sent out a parent survey, I commented on field day and remarked that kinesthetic learners were disenfranchised (a politically correct term I thought may get some real attention, especially in a school where vinyasa is a PE standard). No response. I boycotted until fifth grade when Sharky announced he was "running the mile at field day." There was a new PE teacher and she was more traditional. The yoga lady had retired.

YES! I went. He ran it all right. He led the whole race then got passed at the end. He came in second and threw up in the shrubs. Go Sharky!

My first year teaching at the junior high, I dreaded our field day, but much to my relief, like the new UE PE teacher, MJHS is old school. It turns out that the more rural your school's community, the better the field day is for real athletes. Actually, the football team, who says the Lord's Prayer all the time, is a powerhouse with multiple state titles. See? Further proving that students can have fun, be sporty, talk about Jesus, and learn, the school is also ranked at the top in Tennessee.

My ninth graders had a blast in the hot May sunshine. They sprinted, tossed, bear-crawled, jumped, and tugged with sweat-soaked delight. I was thrilled and asked the principal that day if I could enroll my sons at MJHS, even though we lived in a different county. Students even had a gross eating contest and they cheered each other on, praying someone would throw up. Teachers held the garbage bags. YAY! I learned more about my students in one afternoon of field day than I could in a month of coursework. Good times. Good All-American times.

Still, field day isn't for everyone. After field day, I asked a certain student, "Where were you this afternoon? I didn't see you compete in any events."

She said, "I hid Mrs. Bug. I didn't go to field day and nobody figured it out!" I asked her how she pulled off this feat, and she explained, "Well, when the ninth grade awards ceremony was over, our teacher said to go to the restroom and then meet on the track for ninth grade field day. I just stayed in the bathroom. Then, I waited for the principal to announce *eighth* grade awards day. When I heard the eighth graders walking by the bathroom, I jumped in line."

I was shocked that one of my freshmen angels would be sneaky! "I can't believe you actually *wanted* to sit through eighth grade awards. That had to be so boring" I said.

She answered, "Well, it was better than going outside. Yes, it was boring until the girl sitting right beside me won an award! I freaked out! I just looked straight down at the floor and prayed that no one would recognize me."

I understand that like me many students have anxiety about exercising in public. In my book *Field Day*, character Noah is a nervous wreck but is reassured by his athletic friend. The book's illustrator is a superb athlete from, guess where, EU! I had a competition to find an artist and he won. We kicked off field day at the school once the book was published. The best part is that I got to use the microphone, and here is what I said to all the third-fifth grade students: "Students, I was a terrible athlete who ran high school track for four years. I came in last place in every race I ever ran, but I had fun and stayed in shape. I learned to lose and I learned to admire people who are better at something than I am. Do your best. Be kind to each other. Have fun. That said, I want you to know, young Americans, that it is okay to WIN! Winning is much better than losing!"

I miss teaching and making other people exercise for my entertainment, so I have created the Senior Family Olympics in which Delicious, BBJ, Bop, Gravy, Trout, Terrific, and others will compete for blue ribbons. Obviously, none of them can run anymore, so I adapted events to meet their orthopedic, gastronomical, and vertical situations/skillsets. Following are the events.

1. Park and Bark: Four competitors will start out sitting in one car. At the gun, each will unbuckle, heave him/herself from the car seat, stand outside the vehicle, and shut the door. Anyone who becomes entangled in belts and eyeglass chains will lose points. They must also carry on a conversation the until the last person is out of the car. Anyone who coughs is eliminated.

2. Chairlift: Competitors will rise from easy chairs using only their legs. The first person to the refrigerator wins.

3. Debit or Credit: This is a timed event. Each competitor will visit the grocery store. Once the cashier announces the purchase total, the timer starts. The shopper who finds his/her card, swipes it or inserts it, remembers his/her pin and correctly enters it wins. No checks allowed.

4. No-Bounce Bleacher Crawl: After watching a grandchild's basketball game from the TOP row of the bleachers, each competitor will navigate his/her way to the gym floor without help. Railings are allowed. Stepping from step to step or landing to landing is allowed. This is a game of strategy and balance. Contestants who carry beverages and popcorn sacks get extra points. Anyone who spills either is disqualified.

5. Open Sesame: Competitors will each be given a child's toy that has been shipped from Asia. The package will contain at least ten tiny zip ties keeping individual pieces tight to cardboard and heavy plastic coating encasing the entire toy. Competitors may use a pocketknife, scissors, or steak knife to open the package and remove all zip ties. Anyone who cuts him/herself, breaks the toy, or hides tiny toy pieces will be disqualified.

Trout, the proverbial trash-talker, recently bragged that he is destined to win because, "So far I've been lucky. I've fallen only onto the bed."

Delicious says she know she'll lose and admits, "A month ago, I tripped on my porch and my face landed in the dogfood pan. At least if that happens again and no one finds me for a while, I won't starve."

Relays are out. No one wants to be dragged down by a teammate whose had meniscus surgery and can't hear. Really, the older you get, the smaller your social sphere is anyway, so individual effort is preferable. Ask anyone who has been an adult in graduate school.

Theory 39: Group work is just plain wrong.

M y friend D-Up's college sophomore daughter said, "I hate group projects," to which D-Up replied, "Well, then, you're gonna hate life because this is just an introduction."

It dawned on me last week that I've dreamed my whole life of working alone. Finally, at age 45, I'm there. The dream became a serious goal when I attended grad school and co-taught in the same year. The group effort drained me, and I started scheming for solitude. As I sat through miserable in-service skits by teacher teams and grad school students' group presentations, I experienced my own philosophical epiphany to which many of you will relate: *Group work is just plain wrong.*

My first bad experience with group work occurred my senior year at The University of Tennessee. A finance professor had the prematurely progressive and logistically ridiculous idea to have business students collaborate with art and architecture students on massive, semester-long projects. The architecture students designed and constructed buildings. The finance majors figured out all the numbers. Most of us didn't even have checking accounts at that point, so financing a multi-purpose development was slightly out of reach. My group consisted of three members. Roommate and I covered financial interests and CAD (Covert Architecture Dude) took care of the building stuff. I tag him Covert because we could never find him. Cellphones did not exist. Our schedules did not sync. We couldn't email unless we went to the Humes Hall laundry room or to the library. What was that professor thinking? In other words, that group project was completely inconvenient, over our heads academically, frustrating, and socially awkward. The roommate dynamic is challenging enough. Why add schoolwork to the list of potential fight stimulants? CAD was a problem. He was an old man, well, to Roommate and me anyway. CAD was 25. Even weirder, he and his wife (gross) had a newborn baby. I don't remember what it was; I just remember thinking that being married in college would suck and being married with a baby would double-suck.

As a matter of fact, whenever my college buddies whined about stressful coursework or being dumped, I cheered them up by saying,

"Things could be worse, you know. You could be living in married student housing." That always put things in perspective.

Anyway, Roommate, CAD, and I struggled through that project, but not without injury. I learned that the hardest part of group work is not the *work*ness, it's the *group*ness. That was the ONLY time in college that I visited a professor in his office hours. Pooh had passed away. Delicious and I were flat broke. I figured out a way to graduate a semester early, which would save Delicious (a public school teacher and 49-year-old widow) an important amount of money. I'd also already gotten a job to start in January. We couldn't seem to get the project together and Roommate and I didn't really understand our parts. I was scared, so I saw the professor. I explained to him that the project was wearing me out and that I was afraid it would keep me from passing and graduating. He said one of the most beautiful things I've ever heard a teacher say. Ever. He said, quite fatherly, "I don't fail seniors."

People. *People* make work hard. Group work should really be broken up into individual assignments that align. Partnerships are fraught with stress and embezzlement. Ask anyone in a family business. The dynamics are always the same, especially when siblings are involved. The players may include any of the following: the control freak who wants to run the show because he either has a ridiculous ego or doesn't trust the others, the annoyed sibling who sticks his head in the sand and tries to play peacemaker while his wife begs him to grow a pair, the sister who not only has to perform social gymnastics between everyone but also has to take care of the elderly parents AND work while the brothers make excuses, and the parent who coddles the control freak guy, makes excuses for the sand guy, and expects the sister to understand all the above and deal with it. In any family business, just like any other business, twenty percent of the people do eighty percent of the work. Such dynamics take a toll on relationships. Needless to say, if Tall Child ever wants to work "with" me, he'll be a 1099 Miscellaneous subcontractor.

The hardest group project I ever did was coordinate end of course testing at MJHS. Fortunately, I had an awesome group of women, a room with a lock, and a pair. I laid out the rules on the front end and said, "I am the fall guy for close to 2,000 state exams that must be sorted, administered, proctored, packaged, and shipped without error. I am the boss and you all must do what I ask. This is

NOT a group project. I have joined three teacher unions and am now buying wine by the case. So, help me and I'll share credit like we worked as a group. My team consisted of Red Hot Back Space, Digits, our school attendance secretary who just happens to bring an accounting degree, a seemingly photographic memory, an awesome play list, and a giant bag of candy with her, and Ticonderoga, the fabulously gifted guidance counselor who can count fast, coax coworkers, and cook cobblers. I asked the vice principal why he tasked me with the huge project and he said, "Because you've been a businessperson and won't take any sh*t from the Yankee teachers who work here." Ha! I loved it. My boss gave me permission to be hateful. Perfect.

Sure enough, one of the Yankees challenged me regarding the proctoring plan. She said, "I think we need two teachers in every room. I don't want to be alone."

I asked, "Why? Are you afraid you will tell students the answers?"

She gasped, "No. I just think it's risky."

I explained, "You will be proctoring students in a grade you don't teach who are taking a subject you don't teach. If you have to go to the bathroom, you will text roaming administrators who will relieve you."

She said, "Why can't we have parent volunteers in the room?"

I said, "Because they could be cheaters, perverts, indiscreet morons, annoying, clueless, and so on."

She said, "Well, I don't like you plan."

I said, "Well, you don't have to like anything. Your job is to simply follow my instructions."

That project was one of the most complicated, logistically difficult, high-stakes, nerve-wracking tasks I'd ever attempted, but Red Hot, Digits, and Ticonderoga made it a positive and successful experience. That reminds me of another little group that always seems to appear together: women, stress, and carbohydrates.

Big girl hungry.

On graduate school registration night, I sat with Cool Country Ginger and an exceptionally attractive eighth grade math teacher. Let's call him Hot Math. Someone should send his Olan Mills school picture to the Ford Modeling Agency. Anyway, the moment I sat down, Cool Country Ginger whispered, "Hot Math and I are scoping out potential people we DO want or DO NOT want to work with on group projects. We don't want to get stuck with any weirdos." Yes, strategy is crucial and cannot begin too early. This stuff can get funky, so I have a few coping mechanisms. I follow my "7-Step Group Work Survival System."

STEP 1. Identify the people who live the farthest away so it just doesn't make sense to meet in person. Recruit them early, but only if they aren't stupid.

STEP 2. Identify the person who brought a laptop to registration or to the first class because he/she will likely do the technology. The person who puts all the PowerPoint slides together is kind of like the person who allows the baby or bridal shower to be at her house. She is an equal group member but will do more work because the group is using her turf. I've also noted that MAC users are really excited about their equipment, kind of like breast feeders. They are super eager and want observers to know how awesome Macs and breast milk are, so, well, milk it.

STEP 3. Once the group is assembled, try to take the lead. Yes, that means more responsibility, but it also means you delegate and control the calendar.

STEP 4. Step 4 is a step I TRY to take every day in every group project. Step 4 is "Let the other members be right, even if they might be wrong." Only children may struggle with this step.

STEP 5. Drop the ego. Bring food. If someone else steps up as leader, be prepared to follow orders.

STEP 6: Know that if you come up with a "great idea" you will be responsible for implementing it. For example, a teacher may ask, "What if we write a rap?" She will be the lyricist. Why are any teachers still rapping? I think there's a YouTube learning curve.

Wait a minute. Chocolate?

195

I give a shout-out to my LMU Post-Bacc Realism Project Group from 2009/2010. We had the perfect mix of personalities.

- Me, Bug: I was the interpersonal glue; I injected humor at will to bond our unit. I was also creative.
- County Boy: We grew up together. We had good history, so he trusted me. He trusted me enough that he let us put him in a fake Cialis commercial to teach a philosophy lesson.
- My dear former colleague Tech Savvy is gifted at manipulating software and a diverse mix of individuals to complete a first-class group project that is used as an example for master's level students. See us on the big screen, well, the big *projection* screen, if you can find the jump drive somewhere at the Lincoln Memorial University College of Education in Harrogate, Tennessee.
- Good Sports (two guys). These two were normal men who had great senses of humor and did what Tech Savvy and I told them to do. Nice.
- My dear friend Mother Of The Year Every Year (MOTYEY for short). She is so stinking smart and an incredibly good mama to four children. She knows all about group dynamics. And literature. And grading papers. And the Bible. And coffee. And laundry. And allergies. When I get stressed, I think I'll just put life and group work in perspective by sitting in the lotus pose and whispering, MOTYEY, MOTYEY, MOTYEY.

STEP 7. Be the female leader of an otherwise all-male group.

Expand your notes with this exercise.

A Marital Case Study – Group Work at its Finest?

Each spouse has one brain. Each brain consists of two halves. Remember, there are never more than two halves of anything. I have argued that fact way too many times. The wife uses both halves of her brain in every decision she makes; she attaches emotion and consequence to each cerebral choice. The husband uses primarily (only) the left side of his brain. The dishwasher breaks. In order to save money and please the husband, the wife attempts to fix it. Disaster strikes. She then begs the male, "Do not order a dishwasher at work and recruit some guy you know to install it for a case of beer."

Prompt 1 – Literary analysis: What evidence in this text relates to your life and the claim that group work is inefficient?

Prompt 2 – Mathematical analysis: If the wife uses both hemispheres of her brain and the husband uses only one hemisphere of his brain, can we conclude that the wife is twice as smart as her husband?

Prompt 3 – Psychological analysis: Who is right here? What will happen? Has it happened MANY times before but with different appliances? Can these two individuals actually learn?

The husband says, "Okay. I won't order anything. Geez." The next day, he calls his wife and brags, "You will be so proud of me. I ordered a dishwasher, and my friend said he will install it for a case of beer." Three weeks later a dishwasher arrives at the husband's office. One month after that, he remembers to bring the dishwasher home. Two more months later, he says that his beer friend is divorcing and has a girlfriend out of state, so he's too busy to install the dishwasher.

The wife says, "I told you I wanted to the Sears Outlet. They deliver, install, and haul off the old one."

The husband responds, "Well, I saved us $50. Once so-and-so's divorce is final...."

The wife, whose hands are now raw from scrubbing pots and pans for half the year, throws a wine-induced tantrum. The next day, she is shamed for "getting emotional" about a dishwasher. She sneaks and calls her plumber on the side. That week, the husband arrives home to see an installed dishwasher and a clean kitchen.

He says, "See? I did a good job!"

The next time an appliance breaks, I'm not going to tell Tall Child. I'm going to save up for whatever it is, call my side plumber, order everything, have my side plumber pick up the appliance, install it, and haul off evidence. Group work is just plain wrong. That said, Tall Child is much easier on me than I am on him.

Theory 40: Men are easier to work with than women.

I confess I am a frequent male-basher, but male reader, I love and appreciate you more than you know. I once heard a TV personality say that "Funny women aren't sexy." If you don't think I'm sexy, but you DO think I'm funny, I am honored. It's all good. If Tall Child and I split up, I can't date anyway because I have no outfits worthy of a night out, even to Cracker Barrel before noon. I'm in a real gas station deli fashion mode, and I am so comfortable. As an only child with only one marriage to date (unless you count my fake IRS nuptials to Joe L. in Mississippi—more on that in Theory 42), I relate to male coworkers as brothers. I look to men for guidance, camaraderie, expertise, and humor.

I genuinely enjoy collegiate relationships with men, and I give them space. Female reader, I'm asking now for forgiveness and tolerance as you read. This is your chance to think outside the barn. Hang with me til the end. First, let's make one thing clear. Women have MUCH MORE TO DO every day than men. See figures:

Bug's to-do list

Tall Child's to-do list

I'm not one of those women who doesn't have female friends. I adore my best girlfriends and treasure every moment with them. Honestly, my life would be sad without them. I'm not a jock fly. I have nothing to contribute to sports talk with "the boys." I do not text my friends' husbands. What I'm saying is that I've noticed some major differences in how women behave at work compared to how men behave at work. Men are just easier to work with than women. Shall we work our way up my not-too-impressive resume to explore this Theory?

The Track: I handed out skee ball prizes in the noisy arcade, arranged tiny putters in the golf shack, and docked tourists into the bumper boat mini-marina a couple of summers at The Track in Pigeon Forge, Tennessee. My female teen coworkers whined about the weather. They obsessed over neatness in the ice cream shop. They hated the uniforms. The boys worked on their tans as they dragged entangled cars back on track. They flexed muscle as they rescued spinning fat tourons from the outer edges of the bumper boat pool. Tourists always choke under pressure when it's time to dock. It was the late '80s, early '90s. The boys embraced the polo shirts and accessorized with thick gold chains and flipped collars. The girls gossiped, complained, and tattled. The boys just worked.

IHOP/Assorted other restaurants: I stacked plates, served up sausage, eggs, and pancakes, impatiently guided diners through the menu, and performed miserable side work. For the most part, the servers were female and the management and line cooks were male. The head waitress may just be the meanest job on earth. I'll call my head waitress Leggs because she scolded us when we showed up without our "stockings" on. Who wants to stand in a 100-degree kitchen in panty hose, an apron, a vest, generic high-tops, and, of course, a bow tie? Waitress fights are the best fights because of three elements: 1-dirty soap-opera style romance, 2-nicotine and coffee highs, and 3-the fact that while all the hysterics are playing out, the line cooks (the men who instigated the issues at hand) wheeze with laughter as they stack cured bacon. Oh, and sometimes fights get physical. I was miserable when I was at IHOP because my father had just died. Female Leggs took no pity on me, but male Fry Daddy snuck me special chocolate chip pancakes at the end of every shift.

The Bank: I was a branch manager. My staff consisted primarily of women, most of whom were older than I. Heck, some were even older than Delicious. They were great workers, no doubt, but they argued over the most ridiculous things. I had to referee because Teller A didn't get to take her fibromyalgia medicine with food because Teller B was three minutes late coming back from lunch. By the way, the lunchroom was just a breakroom at the end of the teller line. I asked, "Why didn't you take your medicine anyway?"

Teller A said, "I have to take it at lunch."

I have no medical degree, but I advised her, "I think that means general time of day and with food, not during your bank lunch break." I tried to inspire her by singing, "Eat it Anyway" to the tune of Martina McBride's "Pray it Anyway."

She argued, of course, "Well, the employee handbook says you can't eat in your teller stall." Stall. Appropriate for that one. A man would simply swallow his medicine and say, "Dude, stop being late."

It's true Teller B was problematic. In a confidential annual review, I congratulated her, saying, "Folks all over town know and love you as Mrs. H at the bank. You have a wonderful relationship with our clients, and I appreciate that."

She marched, chin up, waistband *really* up, back to the teller line and said, "Manager Bug just told me that I am the best teller at this branch!"

Once, a co-worker said to me, "Bug, you kinda work like a man."

I said, "Thank you."

School: One early March, two days after the miserable spring forward time change, a couple of female teachers at my school decided our larger team needed to have a 7:45 a.m. (6:45 a.m. body clock time) meeting to discuss ninth grade awards day, which would take place in mid-May. I watched as the women brought up issue after issue and used words like "push back" and "feelings" and asked assorted questions like, "Should we give awards to one boy and one girl in each course or one girl and one boy in each class roster?" and, "What about those kids who aren't good students but are really nice and try hard?" Sleep-deprived and honestly annoyed as the person who not only typed up the awards, but also announced and handed them out on awards day, my workin' man self kicked in.

I said, "Y'all are Obama-ing this event all up. This is an elite school. Each teacher should pick his/her one top student by looking at the grade book. Pick 'em up. Lay 'em down." I scanned the desks to measure response. The guys' faces relaxed as if they'd seen the promised land of the meeting's end. The women's faces contorted with bulging, rolling eyes and cocked heads. Cocked and ready.

~ ~ ~

As usual, I tested this Theory with the future of America, also known as high school freshmen. Today's teenagers are tolerant, open-minded, forgiving, and way more respectful than grown-ups realize. The girls are beyond feminism. To them, Roe V. Wade is a history text. The "glass-ceiling" is some sort of skylight. Equality in the workplace means two days bagging groceries, two days stocking groceries, and one day dragging shopping buggies from the parking lot. I stood in front of my classroom and challenged them, "Okay boys and girls (they may be teenagers, but they love to be called boys and girls), I want to know if you agree. If so, why? If not, why not? Tell the truth. This is a safe place. Men are easier to work with than women."

Hands flagged the stale classroom air. My bold pupils offered up the following statements to back my Theory.

BOYS said:
Women nag.
Men can be persuaded.
Women want to do it perfectly. We just want to do it however we can get it done the fastest then go watch sports.
Women are more expensive, even at jobs.

GIRLS said:
Women like to argue.
Men are easy to control.
I like working with guys because they get out of the way and I can just do everything.

Yes!

I posted the same question to my Facebook page. The responses poured in, but not publicly. Almost every responder sent a private message.

- One friend offered that her ten-year-old son made the following statement: "When girls are together, they fight about things that don't matter and stay mad. Boys have an argument and they forget it about it five minutes later." I agree. I'm also pleased that this young boy notes that boys forget things.

• Another said, "Men gossip as much as women, but women are masters at backbiting then acting like they are your best friends. Men have no clue what's going on. Women know and then [female dog] about the men being clueless. Overall, I prefer working alone!" Preach on, sister.

• "Absolutely men are easier! I've found men either fear me, and we get along great, or they hate me, and we still get along, or they don't understand women and just do as they are told!"

• "Since the ripe old age of 21, I have worked in the same place in a managerial position. I love my job. I couldn't ask for a better boss. He is loyal and generous to his employees and provides a fair work environment, a kind ear, and sage advice to both the staff and clients. But, when my boss retires, I have vowed to never work in a managerial position again. The problem? The women I work with. Personally and individually, they are funny and kind, but as a group they are accusatory, snarky, and a ridiculous bunch of middle school girls, which is funny, in an ironic way, because they are all at least a decade or three older than I am. What the? They whine, they gossip, and they blame each other for mistakes. They gang up on each other and break into teams against each other. Because my boss is loyal, sometimes to a fault, he does not allow anybody to be fired unless she is morally corrupt or criminal, so I am left to herd the cats. I spend half of my job smoothing ruffled fur and determining what really needs to be acted on and what is just snarkiness . . . . In my experience, men don't do this. Grudges aren't held, comments aren't remembered, and they don't cry to their bosses. Middle school girls are hard to live with, but *adult* middle school girls make me want to hurt somebody, usually myself, with an ice pick through my ear drums."

These contributors also reminded me of the almost supernatural element that can overcook anyone's grits: hormones. We all know where testosterone points. Here, we are discussing the particular hormones that women battle to balance. Delicious swears that the Salem Witch trials were just a persecution of menopausal women. Oh, and God bless us, some women get testosterone injections. I took heavy doses of progesterone when trying to conceive. All that did was make me as mean as a striped snake. And fat. Fat just makes us meaner, by the way. Fat and jolly? That's Santa Claus, not me. My friend tagged women as "estrogens" and males as "testosterones." I quote and paraphrase. Here are her observations after numerous years in corporate and philanthropic endeavors:

Estrogens: The competition gets fierce and full of backstabbing and indecisive conversation. No team building, but lots of alliance-making. A woman on a mission is just plain dangerous.

Testosterones: Healthy competition. Men know who the chief is. They know their roles.

Estrogens: Want to know everyone's business.

Testosterones: Get down to business.

Estrogens: A seemingly simple task/project/event snowballs into a cluster mess of needless extra rules and side work. Instead of just leading the committee, estrogens involve other estrogens in decisions, thus mucking up a process. Estrogens yack about where to put a tent.

Testosterones: Erect the tent.

I just remembered that I, Bug, have a medical condition that prevents me from taking female hormone therapy when I hit menopause. Watch your back, Tall Child! To test your new skills, I've prepared an assessment.

I asked Sharky, age seventeen as I wrote this, "Who works harder—men or women?"

He said, "Men work physically harder and don't get onto you as much. Women work mentally harder, but women think too much."

Theory 41: In the Christmas season, men need to do as they are told.

Usually, about December 20, I freak because I am in the red zone with no play to run. I do love holidays, just like I love Pampered Chef products, but boy do all the preparations and expenses take a toll on me. Plus, holidays bring intense thoughts that further scatter my brain. Someone else has died. I grieve for the paper inhabitants of the Angel trees. I feel guilty for being a church heathen. My heart aches for men and women still trying or waiting to become parents. Women connect it all: left brain lists, obligations, and responsibilities, and right brain emotions, attitudes, and energy. Having too much to think about and to do makes me sad and mad. I direct my anger toward men in general, and from what I've heard in bank breakrooms and teacher lounges, I'm not the only Mrs. Claus who grows claws at Christmas. I am the Grinch of Glen Cove subdivision, well, except for his svelte shape. Worn out women should be focused on the birth of Christ, not hypocritically singing "You'd better not pout, you'd better not cry, you'd better not shout."

What if. WHAT IF Tall Child and I did one of those *Freaky Friday* movie swap situations where he becomes responsible for EVERYTHING and I just eat Rotel and watch TV? What if Tall Child found the lights and lit our house ablaze while I said, "Oooh?" What if Tall Child walked down into the woods, unscrewed the tree stand from last year's tree, brought it back, screwed it to the new tree, strung the lights, and dragged ornaments out of the filthy guest room closet, all the while fighting an asthma attack that would develop into a sinus infection, as I simply observed and said, "What are you cooking for supper? Make something festive."

We women can't just toss out some red and green objecto de` artos. Oh, noooooo. We must create magical, mystical, battery and electronically powered worlds. Actually, we must create *experiences* that awaken and entertain all the senses, at once, every moment of every day for at least 30 straight days. Homes look like the inside of a snow globe. The Christmas to-do list is monumental, complex, and IMPORTANT.

Honestly, have you ever heard anyone say, "I can't believe [insert man's name] didn't put up a Christmas tree yet" or "[Man's name], have you bought any Christmas presents?" or "Hey, [man's name], which Christmas Eve service are y'all attending?" To illustrate, listen to the conversation I had one December week with Fancy, who is a world-renowned specialist in her field, university professor, and mother of three boys:

Day: Saturday
Time: 9:30 a.m.
Location: Elementary school gym back row so we can lean our aching bodies against the cinderblock wall and not lose our pocketbooks through the bleacher gaps

Bug: *We drove by your house last night and booed you because your tree wasn't on.*
Fancy: *I don't have a tree.*
Bug: *What? It's the middle of December. Better get with it, Fancy.*
Fancy: *[Expletive], I have not had one minute to get a tree.*
Bug: *Can you get one today?*
Fancy: *[Expletive], my three boys have six basketball games today.*

It never occurred to me to ask the father, The Gentleman, who was sitting right beside me, if HE had bought a tree. He just sat there eating popcorn, watching the ballgame, dreaming of a white Christmas. Men do care. Tall Child, as his nickname should imply, LOVES holidays. Last Halloween, I hit five stores to assemble Sharky's zombie-fighting Rick Grimes *Walking Dead* costume, fought Gnome into his football player costume, bought candy, found reflective tape, assembled glow necklaces for dozens of children, and packed my trick-or-treating cooler. Tall Child followed the hay wagon full of children from house to house. One year he rolled a yard. Well, actually, he panicked and rolled a tree. I did create Christmas jobs for Sharky and Gnome. Sharky waters the tree or doesn't. I don't really care. Gnome gets the mail so that I am shielded from all the Christmas cards and don't feel guilty for not reciprocating. Each year, fewer and fewer cards arrive.

When Gnome was about four, I brought the tree in and set it upright. He yelled, "Yay! Now turn it on!" Maybe it's time to farm out more work and get the plastic pre-lit deal.

Proud boy

Let's break this Theory down by the senses, then further break it down by traditional gender responsibilities. This may reek of Southern female submission, but, hey y'all, we love our big ol' strappin' men.

SOUND
Women: We hear screaming hyper children and wrangle them. We tolerate Santas and rocking Rudolphs on our counters, which means we also have to unplug and replug the toys to open soup cans for casserole ingredients. We carol and force our children to carol. When carolers come to the door, we listen and force our children to listen, while men hide in their recliners. What happens if the Domino's guy comes to the door while the carolers are singing? Should he join in? Should we tip everybody? We hear glass

ornaments hit hardwood. Then we hear ourselves sweeping said glass into dust pans.

Men: Men hear themselves crack walnuts that women leave in festive dishes on coffee tables. Men hear ESPN Gameday.

SMELL
Women: We light evergreen and apple spice candles. We lean cinnamon-infused brooms from Kroger against entry walls.

Men: Say, "Oooh, something smells gooood."

TOUCH
Women: Buy, wrap, lift, hide, and deliver gifts in a thousand directions: daycare, school, church, coaches, hostess gifts, secret Santa office parties, God-forbid cookie exchange, friends who say they won't buy one and do (so confusing), and family. Then you have the gift matrix: Gnome to Sharky, Sharky to Gnome, Tall Child to Gnome and Sharky, Gnome and Sharky to Tall Child, Bug to Gnome and Sharky, Sharky and Gnome to Bug, Bug to Tall Child, Tall Child to Bug (we hope), then exponentialize all this to Delicious and Bop and cousins and exchange names? I am so confused. The Recession actually helped me out. Did anyone else out there start drawing names during the economic downturn? Don't go back to the matrix just because the economy is better. Please.

Men: Ripping paper. No bags for my guy. Tall Child prefers presents wrapped in tissue, encased in boxes, wrapped in pretty paper, tied with ribbons that require scissors. It's an *experience*, remember? He's okay with a T-shirt and his annual one-a-day devotional calendar as long as they are wrapped this way.

I took a break from Christmas cards for a few years. But, after we brought home Gnome, understandably, Tall Child begged me to send photo Christmas cards. I pitched a hissy fit and demanded he at least stamp and mail the envelopes. Well, he stamped them but on the top left corner of all 200 envelopes. I pitched a hissy fit sequel and said, "People are going to think I don't know how to put a stamp on an envelope, and I teach business education! And I'm a writer!"

Tall Child argued, "I did it."

I argued back, "Nobody will think that you addressed the cards."

Tall Child went to the post office and asked a clerk for clarification, called me, and said "No problem. Stamps work anywhere. Cards are going out today. No delays. That's right. Who's your daddy?"

Christmas cards from people who have time and money

TASTE:

Women: We hit the grocery store one thousand and one times. We bake cookies and simmer fragrant dishes for our families, other families, office parties, our husbands' office parties, for our mothers, our mothers-in-law, potlucks, you get it. And we figure out ways to carry it all without ruining our work and doling out food poison.

Men: Eat.

SIGHT:

Women: We create and foster the experience. Then, we create miniature experiences within the experience, like Christmas villages and nativity sets. We also design the system. Glass ornaments up high. Stuffed animals down low. Lights in front of windows. Something shiny for each neighbor. Appropriately spaced candy dishes, nutcrackers, Santa collections. And so on. And, of course, we monitor and protect all the above. I'm losing my grip. Joseph went for a Jeep ride, wrecked, and did not recover. Jesus is flat out missing. The last I saw him he was wrapped in swaddling clothes and hiding under a bedspread with some pumpkin cookie crumbs.

Men: Say, "This looks awesome! I love Christmas!"

An aerial view of an experience within an experience

Thanks for the thumbs up, S.C., but I need to work on scale.

Let us "recall, the most famous [sense] of all". It is the Sixth Sense, one of spirits. I have to confess. I am terrified I'll forget about Santa Claus. Not only do I have to ensure that the original legend is protected, but I also—dad gum it—created my own mythical tasks back when I was a relatively stress-free housewife hopped up on Andre champagne and cranberry juice. Now I have to be you-know-who AND make sure you-know-who eats cookies, drinks milk, and wipes his dirty boots on the rug I place in front of the fireplace after I remember to open the fireplace door. At least he won't get burned because the fireplace hasn't worked in twenty years. Then I have to make sure Sharky and Gnome leave a Christmas card for you-know-who and later write him a thank-you note. Shoot. I usually forget to have them write the Dear Santa letter. Last year, I asked sixteen-year-old Sharky to write one for both of them. That was a big help and Tall Child even stamped and mailed it.

Don't even get me started on the *Elf on a Shelf* book and doll conundrum. Ca-ching and congrats to the mother who thought up that tale and book and doll and merchandizing. You suck. Gnome named his elf Blarg. He bought the story hook, line, and sinker.

211

Unfortunately, I'm not the best at leveraging legends. One winter day I said, "Gnome, you are acting ugly. You'd better straight up because Blarg can see you."

Gnome said, "No he can't. He's in the other room."

Last year, Gnome and his buddy Pac-Man found our elf in my underwear drawer. Yes, that's disturbing on two fronts, but the aggravating front is the dang elf. They brought him to me, wrapped in a towel because technically you can't touch the Elf or he loses his stupid magic, in the living room. Pac-Man excitedly yelled, "We found the elf! And it's just the first week of December! But Gnome said he hasn't read the story yet. How'd his elf get here if you haven't read the story?" You must read the book one night and then the elf appears the next morning to monitor your child's behavior. He flies back to the North Pole every the night and reports to Santa. Then he flies back to your house and lands in a new location to continue judgement. Gnome and Pac-Man were eight and curious, so I had to think fast.

I said, "Oh, helk, that's an old Norwegian toy that is made to look like the *Elf on a Shelf*. That's not Blarg. I've had that little toy my whole life."

"What? He looks just like my elf from last year," Pac-Man questioned.

"No, no," I said. "Just an old toy. I think the lady who wrote *Elf on a Shelf* used those toys for models. Yep, that's exactly what she did."

Later that night, Gnome brought me the book and said, "Let's read it. I want my elf to come tonight while I'm asleep."

"Okay," I said. I read it all cuddly-wuddly-snubble-wubbikins. Then I asked, "Where did you and Pac-Man put my toy Norwegian elf."

"We hid it," he said.

The mood shifted. I thought, *Oh, [expletive]. What am I going to do between now and tomorrow morning about this [expletive] elf?* I jumped on Amazon and ordered one for Prime shipping, but that left me [expletive] out of luck for the next morning. I had to cover with more lies. The next morning, Gnome scurried around the house looking for Blarg. I said, "Oh, he's here somewhere. I bet he has learned how to be extra stealth at hiding from us." Dishonest? Necessary.

Theory 42: Don't blog about women woes. You'll tempt fate with your secret boyfriend and the IRS.

Christmas break 2013 was not a break for me. I savor every day off. It probably sounds weird to you, since I'm a self-employed writer, but I have many wonderful clients and I actually do have to schedule vacation time. Entrepreneurs have a hard time not working at all during any day. Writing down "Vacation Day" helps. I want the old glorious feelings of anticipating nothingness. Two parts of days off make me especially happy. The first part is early morning when I open my eyes and start mentally checking off my working mother to-do list and realize that I—yee-haw—don't have to work that day. I actually get up extra early on those mornings to extend my vacation. The second is late evening (for me 9:00 p.m.), when I start my person to person, bag to bag, ready for school-daycare-work tomorrow inventory and realize that I—yee-haw—don't have to drive anyone anywhere the next morning.

I was a teacher back in 2009. I was busy and tired, and I was really looking forward to a nice long break where I could read to Gnome, watch Sharky's basketball games, entertain family, eat and drink at will, and watch Hallmark movies. But, as my not-so "Tender Tennessee Christmas" unfolded, I learned a big lesson: Don't blog about brother-husbands or women doing all the work. You'll tempt fate. Boy, did I tempt fate when I published preliminary drafts of "Theory 19: All mothers need sister wives." Often, I toss paragraphs into cyberspace to see if they boomerang back with comments and applause. I wrote:

> *I've tried to beat myself home before so I could welcome me to a clean house and supper on the stove, but even Big Red can't drive that fast. Where's* my *heavy duty help? Sometimes I want to be nurtured, to point and delegate, to get in the luge position and watch Bravo. Well, one uterus seems to equal no dice. I need another uterus to help me. Or maybe uteri? Can I get an "amen" from the sisterhood?*

... but I'm not sure I could live with a bunch of women. I think I'd rather have brother husbands. I could assign them domestic regions of responsibility and choose them according to skill! I'd marry one plumber, one electrician, one handyman, one pediatrician, one academic, one party boy, one financial expert, and one family man."

Basically, I complained that men don't do enough and women have to do too much and questioned that perhaps I need an additional man. Well, it turns out I have one. I tempted fate and found a mate! I would like to introduce y'all to my second husband. No, wait, Tall Child and I are still married, so let me rephrase. I'd like to introduce y'all to Tall Child's brother husband, Joe L. My CPA Fairway Tax is a patient golf-fanatic and conservative accountant. He called me at school in November of 2013 to tell me that Tall Child's and my joint tax returns for 2011 and 2012, which we'd filed electronically, were rejected by the IRS. Fair(way) Tax asked me, "Do you know a guy named Joe L.?"

I said, "No, why?"

Fairway Tax said, "Well, the IRS says y'all are married."

I cussed a blue streak—not at Fairway Tax, of course, but the IRS, the tax code, humanity, Tall Child (though he had nothing to do with this), and men in general. Once the fatherly Fairway Tax talked me off the ledger, I did what all working mothers do. I started taking care of business.

My first Christmas vacation weekday, I paid Sharky $20 to brother-sit Gnome as I waited for, then spoke to, an IRS agent on the phone for two hours. I found out that somehow Joe L. got my Social Security number and my 2011 W-2 from Knox County Schools. Needless to say, Joe L.'s and my marital relationship soon birthed a bulging notebook full of correspondence between our clergy (the IRS) and me. In my letter to the IRS, I wrote:

I included screen printouts of what I found. I hope that helps you solve this mystery. I do have a question: Should I file a police report? I hesitated to do so initially, hoping that the mix-up was clerical, not criminal. Also, am I accruing tax penalties? If so, will they be waived once this situation is cleared up? And, is the IRS investigating this fraud and will you file charges against Mr. Joe L.?

I spent five minutes online and found Joe L.'s address. I hope that helps. Please advise.

The IRS responded with a whopping, "We received your correspondence" correspondence letter. No answers. No results. Really? My and Joe L.'s book baby got so chubby! In mid-December, the IRS did send me a sweet little note saying an Identify Theft Fraud Alert had been placed on my account, but there was nothing I could do. That didn't stop them from giving MY money away! During Christmas break, I opened *another* letter from the IRS stating that thousands of dollars (my 2012 tax refund) was direct deposited. Somewhere out there. The letter asked, "Did you get this refund? If not, complete the enclosed forms." Yay, me. Down went another hour on the phone and an afternoon compiling more evidence of my honesty.

One letter I haven't written is a love letter to my brother husband Joe L. Writing is cathartic, my day was shot, so I went ahead with it.

Dear Joe L.,

I miss you baby! Even more, I miss my money that you stole that I owe to other people. But, I suppose this is one of the "worse" times. I'm sure we'll work it out. It's cold here in Tennessee. How are you spending the tax refund? Building a deck? Buying a boat? Oh, enough chit chat. We need to sync our calendars. I need you. Mississippi is too far away. Tall Child has to work this weekend and Sharky has seven basketball games, so you should come up and wash his uniforms. Buy a case of Powerades, too. Also, Sharky's buddy is spending the night Saturday night. You can stay up late with them. I have a movie to watch. Speaking of, please get me some Pinot Grigio on your way here. Hmmm. A magnum. Oh, and, Tall Child's car is in the shop. Unless you know how to fix a water pump, we need you to at least take OUR tax refund that YOU deposited and pay for the repairs. If only you were closer, baby, I could hit you in the face with a skillet.

XOXOXO
Your Bug

Basically, my Christmas plate was full. Throughout December, I procrastinated every grown-up thing I needed to do, including the IRS romance stuff, until my break—a two week span in which time would crawl and I would efficiently get stuff done and get ahead. I made a giant to-do list for my side gig writing projects, magazine articles, guest blog posts, holiday fun, bills, entertaining, gift-buying, Joe L., you name it! Yay. Break. NOT.

Sharky and I got out of school Friday, December 20. We went straight to Walmart to gobble up lots of cheap thoughtful gifts for friends and family. Check! We hit the grocery store. Check! We went to a party that night. Check! We were off to a great red and green start! Saturday, Sharky played in four basketball games and I went *back* to Walmart, this time with Delicious, so we could sneak presents for Sharky and Gnome. Then we went to Hobby Lobby. I survived. She thrived. Check. Sunday, more basketball games. Monday, Sharky, Gnome, and I headed out around 10:30 a.m. to buy more groceries and run final errands. When we got home at 2:30 p.m., I walked into the kitchen to see my little jewelry box turned over on the kitchen table and the sliding glass door handle on the ground outside. GULP. I grabbed Gnome and yelled for Sharky to go back to the car immediately! I said, "We've been robbed and he may still be here. Hurry! Get out!" (Yes, I am certain the robber was male.)

We rushed into Big Red. I cranked her up and backed her around to face my front door. My hope was that the robber would run across the driveway and I could hit him. With my car. Seriously. Maybe I've been watching too much *Walking Dead*. Whatever. I was calm and ready to put pedal to metal and thief to pavement. I called 911 and waited. I called Tall Child who asked, immediately, "Did he steal the TV?" Panic time.

The robber took, as they always do, peace of mind and items that have no material value and all kinds of sentimental worth. I told Tall Child that the robber took my grandmother's engagement bracelet, my grandfather's Navy bracelet, and other heirloom costume jewelry. I cried a little. A seemingly unflustered Tall Child said, "Well, Bug, it's only jewelry. I'm just thankful that you and the boys didn't walk in on him." I marveled at his calm response. Too soon. About an hour later I heard Tall Child scream, "That [expletive] took my leaf blower!" Then, when he sat down to watch TV, I heard him say, what the [expletive] is wrong with the cable?"

I explained, "The robber cut wires to our internet, cable, phone, and old alarm system."

Tall Child yelled, "Doesn't that [expletive] guy know it's bowl season?"

Loooooong story short, I spent the rest of my Christmas break in increments of 8:00 a.m. to 12:00 pm or 1:00 p.m. to 5:00 p.m. with service workers from AT&T, Comcast Cable, Champion Window and Door, Knox County Sheriff's deputies, forensics, a detective, and, finally ADT. Then AT&T, again, then the insurance company, then Champion, again.

Who says students don't need to master informational text?
This was my holiday reading material!

My valuables are gone forever.. As far as Tall Child's leaf blower goes, well, maybe Joe L. can buy us a new one. He can certainly afford it. At least I had the skillset and time off to take care of everything. The robbery rattled me, but I am strong. Mamas do the hard stuff, and we do it well.

Theory 43: When Mama's out of commission, the world falls apart.

I rolled out of bed one Monday morning with a dehydration-style pounding headache, stuffed, itchy, dripping nose, watery eyes, and sinus pain. I did the lovely neti-pot routine and operated as normal. The long drive to work was stressful and the school day interminable. Tuesday, I caved and called the substitute teacher hotline. I also called the doctor even though I suspected a simple bad cold that wouldn't be treatable by prescription. I went for broke because I didn't have time to be sick. As my mother-in-law put it once, "I have to be okay because too many people depend on me."

Can I get an amen from the sister wives, mothers, and especially single mothers? The kind doctor pitied me and wrote a prescription for enough steroids, antihistamine, nasal spray, and Amoxicillin "to get me through the rest of the school year" in case I got worse and didn't have time to come back to the doctor. I had a similar experience with Sharky's ear, nose, and throat doctor, Super Sweet Doctor Daddy. I would tell you that he's father to two of my best friends, but there are rules. The first time I visited him with Sharky I said, "You know, Dr. SSDD, I'm buddies with Flower Child and Elaine." They are his daughters and their pictures were hanging on the examining room wall. He said, "Oh, I can't talk about that. HIPAA." He respects the rules of his profession. He respects women. After examining Sharky, Dr. SSDD turned to me and asked, "What can I do for Mama while you are here?" I was startled.

"The appointment is just for Sharky."

Dr. SSDD said, "Well, Mama is the doctor in the house. If she's not well, everyone and everything in the family is disrupted. We need to keep Mama well." After a confession-like conversation, I walked away with a prescription for Ambien and a one-day cure for yeast infections. Dr. SSDD said, "Say you are on a beach trip and one of you girls gets a yeast infection. With this pill, you can be her new best friend." He communicated such respect for my role as wife and mother. I was so touched; I literally cried all the way home. I wanted, desperately, to tell my friends about the experience, but I didn't want to break the doctor's privacy policy.

I conjured up this Theory while man-handling Gnome in one of my usual hangouts, the basketball gym, where Sharky attempts his Elliot-on-a-bicycle flights to the hoop for two-point floaters. My buddies Stat Mama and Yacht Daddy were sitting beside me in the bleachers. They were all caught up in an intense logistical debacle. Stat Mama had a business trip to the West Coast. Yacht Daddy anticipated an entire week at home with two boys. The boys were twelve and ten at the time. The family lives way out on the lake, really far from work and school, so they bought a tiny yacht and keep it parked at a marina in downtown Knoxville. A few days before Stat Mama was telling me about her logistics puzzle, the ten-year-old tripped on his backpack as he skipped backward down the dock and did the Nestea plunge into an icy cold Tennessee River. Yacht Daddy rushed to the edge of the dock, laid flat on the boards, reached down and fished out a shivering, soaked boy by his backpack straps.

The family splits time between the house and the boat while they also navigate school, work, and busy sports commitments. Daily schedules aren't simple. Laundry is a nightmare. I observed, as I love to do in any basketball gym, the human condition. I studied both parents as they planned out the coming week. As Stat Mama repeated and rehearsed with Yacht Daddy, I watched beads of sweat dot his middle-age forehead. Yacht Daddy is no dummy. He's basically a chief financial officer for a huge organization and supervises hundreds of people. He's a smart, competent, cheerful, loving father. But, he is a man. And as we women on the bleacher back row watched them converse all weekend long about what he needed to do Monday, Tuesday, Wednesday, Thursday, and Friday, we just shook our heads and prayed for sanitary meals, homework completion, dry walks to the car, and Stat Mama's peace of mind on the other side of the country.

When women are ill, out of town, post-surgery, post-partum, etc., friends drop off casseroles, bring flowers, and babysit for them. When men are ill, out of town, post-surgery, post-partum, most folks do nothing because a wife/mother/sister/girlfriend is handling things. Really think about it. When is the last time you took a casserole to a man with a wife? We only show up with our 9x12 pans when the FEMALE is close to death or dead. Red Hot Backspace, Dogwood Debutante, each of whom have been

219

successful professionals and single mothers, and I weighed in on this topic. I can't thank them enough. We offer up a mixed bag of all that goes awry when Mama is out of commission. Do you agree?

- Groceries spontaneously disappear.
- Children come into the "sick" room. Constantly. With basketballs. Stay out!
- Men and children email, text, and call with every issue that comes up. Ironically, they do so with issues they handle fine on their own when Mama is *not* sick or *not* out of town. I asked Tall Child, "What are you only interested in what I have to say when I have laryngitis?"
- We hear, "Don't bother Daddy; he's on the phone." But it never matters when Mama is in meetings, in front of a class, laid up in bed, on the phone, or asleep. Men and children talk to sleeping women as though they are actually awake. What's sad is that women answer them.
- Children come to Mama. Period. Gnome will be sitting in Tall Child's lap and still yell down the hall for me to fix him a peanut butter and jelly sandwich.
- Daddy may take children out to eat, but nutrition is out the drive-thru window. "He had potatoes and bread and nuggets. That's great!"

- Lunch boxes are filled with neon or beige vitamin-free food like Cheez-its, gummies, cereal, and Pop-Tarts.
- Sibling unrest escalates into war and medical bills. The walls shake. The pictures crash. Mama has to referee lying down.
- Sharpies magically appear and artwork shows up on the walls. In. Every. Room. Of. The. House. And on windows and furniture. And somehow in the car.
- The movie *Toy Story* comes to life. Really. One thousand toe-stumping toys scatter across kitchen counters and living floors while some even land in the toilet. This phenomenon continues with board games. Mama, if you feel a headache coming on, do yourself a favor. Lock up Monopoly and Candyland or you'll be on your knees digging dusty Community Chest cards from under the sofa forever.

At least Gnome's color choices matched the chair.

- No one flushes and no one changes the toilet paper roll. Unless the toilet is full of Legos. Then someone flushes. Many times, he flushes.

- When Mama is well and out of town, the children automatically get sick. Automatically! Then, Mama is answering phone calls from Dallas, Texas, and making appointments, directing Daddy to the doctor's office, then checking back to make sure Daddy gave kiddo medicine after his lunch of Fruit Loops and soda crackers.
- When Mama is sick all dishes are dirty. Everything is missing. The blankies are 40 miles away at Grandmama's. There are no garbage bags or clean towels in the house.
- When Mama works up the energy to drive herself to the doctor, the car is out of gas. Actually, the teenager's car is out of gas and her car is at West High School.
- Bedtime is always late and a fiasco. It's funny how dinner/homework/bath time/bedtime can run so smoothly when Mama is okay but become a nightmare when Mama is out of commission.
- Daddy absentmindedly exposes children to scary and or sexy movies, gives them routine-wrecking naps, and feeds them energy drinks. Then, the children get out of whack and throw up in their beds. Then they throw up in Mama's bed as they ask her questions while she sleeps.
- Children are late to school with clothes that don't match/teeth not brushed/homework not done/no lunch. Children call Mama. Mama calls Daddy. It ain't pretty. He has no clue how to add money to an online lunch account and can't figure out how to access her spreadsheet that contains every website ever, along with hyperlinks, descriptions, usernames, and passwords.
- When my cousin was sick, she directed her husband Coach Bama to handle dry-cleaning. She let him have it when she saw her Walmart nightshirt in a plastic cleaning bag with a $4.50 receipt pinned to the $5 shirt's shoulder.
- After his beloved wife of 60+ years passed away, Delicious's grandfather asked her, "Where are the knives?" He also almost burned the house down because he started a skillet of fried pork chops and "let them cook" while he went to check on the cows.
- If I get sick, Tall Child starts coughing. If I limp, he limps.

~~~

222

In one of my pity-party working mama meltdowns, I challenged Tall Child that he was not doing enough housework. My go-to phrase is, "I am overwhelmed."

He said, "I help a lot."

I hissed a list complete with statistical data. I prefer to complain in dramatic detail with stats to back up my claims.

I asked, "You think you help a lot?"

"Yes, I do."

"I do things here that you can't even imagine. Have you ever even looked at the spreadsheet?"

"I know it's there. And, I do the floors too. You forget about that."

"When is the last time you cleaned the floors?"

"Last year when Mom came at Christmas."

Delicious isn't a fan of this Theory, even though she admits she thinks everything I've written here is true. She says I'm hard on Tall Child. I just know she is smitten with my husband. I'm not a male-basher at all. *I love men.* Women simply need more help. Feminists should have pushed for more assistance on the household front before getting women entrenched in the workplace. In other words, we needed to be liberated before we were liberated. Instead, many of us are now expected to work like modern men and keep house like their mothers. I much prefer spending my energy on academic and creative pursuits than I do loading a dishwasher. Recently, I proposed to Tall Child that we take slips of paper and write different yuck household tasks on each one. Then, we could draw from a hat. You draw it, you do it. He said, "Okay. Go ahead and get the papers and make the lists and find a hat and put everything in the hat and we'll see what happens."

Men need us, but we need each other even more. Be likeable, and while you're at it, work on making your children likeable.

Theory 44: Mama's behavior determines how well other folks like her baby.

Have you ever offended a new mother? Have you ever been offended *by* a new mother? Were *you* an offensive new mother? It is crucial that other people like your children because you *will* be out of commission, and you *will* need help. Alienate others by raising obnoxious or untouchable children and you isolate yourself.

Please know I do not consider myself a behavioral expert. I doubt my parenting skills daily. I have failed my children in countless ways thus far, but most of the time they appear to like me. The only green vegetable Gnome eats is the leaves of strawberries. Sharky has narrowed his college choices down much differently than I would have expected years ago. He told a recruiter, "I will go to any state and attend a college any size as long as I can play basketball and the town has good restaurants like Zaxby's." We are irregular church goers. Sharky is terrified of being forced into a Sunday school scavenger hunt. Gnome is a night owl so getting him up on Sunday mornings is miserable for everyone. Tall Child fakes like he has to go to the bathroom every time we are supposed to "pass the peace" (greet people in neighboring pews). I just don't like wearing real clothes. We don't eat dinner as a family, either, but we are still a family. I make all kinds of mistakes, but one thing I try hard to get right is helping Sharky and Gnome build their own mutually respectful relationships with friends and family.

Reader, I'm assuming you are alone right now in your office, classroom, car, or living room. We can be honest here, right? I want you to relax, close your eyes, and think of a child whom you should be close to and enjoy, but you just don't like him/her as you expected to. Upsetting, isn't it? Weird, right? Now, concentrate on the child. See the child holding an adult hand and follow that hand up an arm, over a shoulder, up a neck. Do you see a face? Whose face do you see? The mother? Yep. It's not the child's fault you find him annoying, odd, or unsettling. It's the mother's fault.

I figure I'll get some hate mail on this Theory. As always, I dug around among my friends for fodder, but I'm not naming names or assigning blame! I'll take one for the team because any mama who committed the offenses I'm about to illustrate probably didn't mean to. You were pregnant, a new mother, raising a toddler, rearing a young child, and you missed something important, likely out of shock and exhaustion at the responsibility of keeping another human alive. That said, you failed to set your child up for social acceptance among your adult friends and family, which really stinks for your adult friends and family because they truly love your child and desire a one-on-one relationship with him/her. It also stinks for you because you've put yourself on Untouchable Island. For the pregnant reader, take heed. Avoid what my aunt Terrific calls "bad baby etiquette."

My uncle Gravy's father said something long ago that made so much sense. He said, "Other people have to like your child too."

It is okay to spoil a Yorkie. Only the owner has to love the dog, but no one likes a yappy child. So, how does a new mother accomplish this task? Why, by her own behavior. Of course, she can't always control her baby/toddler/child, but she absolutely can control herself. Let's examine this Theory in three phases.

Phase 1: Pregnancy

"Instead of wishing away nine months of pregnancy and complaining about the shadow over my feet, I'd have cherished every minute of it and realized that the wonderment growing inside me was to be my only chance in life to assist God in a miracle.
—Erma Bombeck, "If I Had My Life to Live Over"

Check yourself, pregnant girl. Others' attitudes toward your child start in gestational week one. When you see two pink lines, don't text the news to close relatives and buddies. Anyone who is going to love the child merits at least a phone conversation. Don't

225

be high maintenance. You can sit in the backseat unless you are full of triplets.

Be thankful, not petty and spoiled. When a certain hen I knew was expecting her first chick, she clucked relentlessly. Tall Child compared, "You know, Bug, when you were pregnant with Sharky, you didn't act like that. It was like you were never even pregnant." I took that as a compliment. I guess his 40-pound weight gain kept him from noticing my 55-pound weight gain and twelve-hour naps. I suppose I was more hog than hen. Plus, I was at work all day.

When folks ask you about your due date, the sex, the nursery, be sweet. They are simply taking an interest or don't even care and are just being polite. Don't be all secretive and snooty. Exercise patience by listening intently to other mamas' labor stories. They are trying to bond with you in the motherhood club and start a relationship with the baby. Visualize a friend talking to your child four years later, "I remember when your mama was pregnant. We were all so excited." Trust me; you'll be just as repetitive, boring, and annoying someday.

Please refrain from rubbing and scratching your belly. Gross. I itch too, but I try not to scratch in public. Hide behind a clothing rack.

Let baby shower hostesses decide how many invitations hit the post office. Don't pressure friends to go broke by inviting people you haven't seen in years. When a kind soul throws you a baby shower, remember your goal is to collect booties, not loot. When you ask for too much stuff, people may dread what drama and elitism you will birth along with your baby. Pregnancy may fatten your rear, but it does not by default fatten your friends' wallets. Be thoughtful with your gift registry; mix up the items by price. Build respect for your growing family by showing respect to those who will love the baby and can't afford a movie star stroller. I recently heard of a girl who actually has a "stroller fund" because she registered for a $900 dollar carriage. Really? Junior high teachers would have to throw a school dance to come up with that kind of money.

Remember, you set the tone for any party that is thrown in your honor. No person is really dying to watch you open gifts until you open the gift she brought. Move quickly, speak up, laugh, smile, pass the sweet pink and blue fluffy loveys (what are those, anyway?)

around. Demonstrate appreciation to faithful attendees who wreck their low-carb diets on iced petit fours smack dab in the middle of their days off.

Use your manners, girls. In the South we have legendarily explicit instructions for thank you notes. The important thing is to write them. Please. If you don't take the time to thank someone who chipped $50 dollars into the stroller fund, how do you think she'll feel? "It just ain't fittin'."

Be gracious to those who come to the hospital, especially older relatives who wait all day eating Bugles and sipping Coke as they stiffly sit on mauve pleather. Everyone who waits at the hospital should get to see and ideally hold the baby after he or she is born. That same day/night. Tell that mean nurse trying to force you to breastfeed to chill for a second so everyone can meet the baby they've mentally labored and prayed over for nine months and twelve hours.

Phase 2: Infancy

> "The thing that impresses me most about America is the way parents obey their children." —Edward VIII

If you ever say, "Shhh" to a grown-up, shhhame on you! Children should cater to adults, not the other way around. I literally typed that after giving Gnome my cell phone so he could play strange digital golf games and dipping him a second bowl of ice cream. Do as I say, ... If, for some insane reason, you must bring a baby to a tailgate, or if your baby must nap while people are watching a ballgame on TV, don't ask any adults to curb their behavior. If you are worried about cooties, stay home.

People relate to and start loving your child when they are *allowed* to relate to and love your child. I took an eight-day-old Gnome to one of Sharky's baseball games. Sharky and his eight-year-old teammates begged to hold baby Gnome. I asked the boys to sit cross-legged on the ground. They actually got in a line to wait for their turns! Each boy held Gnome and, to this day, each boy loves Gnome. Groups of them will shout his name when he prances into a sporting venue. Gnome is to gyms and ballfields as Norm is to *Cheers*.

Gnome makes friends at the ball park.

For the love of Similac, don't be a nap Nazi. If I can sleep anywhere—band bus, football stadium, classrooms, movie theaters, restaurant booths—so can a baby who mostly sleeps anyway. Babies love to be held. Friends love to hold babies! When your buddy, your coworker, a sweet church lady or friend of your mother-in-law spends the time, effort, and money to cook and bring you a casserole, let her into your house. As a matter of fact, hand her the baby. Dig through the goody basket to pile up a plate full of everything she brought. Let her rock the baby and talk to you and watch you enjoy her considerate gift. If she gave the baby an outfit, dress him in it the next time you will see her. She'll feel appreciated and trusted. And, she'll feel important and connected to the child. If the baby is asleep, get the baby out of the bed so she can rock him/her.

Know your baby's role in society.
- Church: Go nursery or go home. Let that baby build blocks for Jesus!
- Wedding: Go hallway or go home. Babies are the worst wedding crashers. A shrill shriek in the middle of The Lord's Prayer? Sacrilegious!
- Funeral: The last time I attempted a funeral with Gnome, he asked me to take him to the concession stand.

Phase 3: Toddlerhood into Childhood

"A person's a person, no matter how small." —Dr. Seuss

I find it ironic that a woman will fall in love with a man yet disagree with his mother's parenting style. That bride will vow to spend her entire life with a man who is a product of an upbringing that she thinks was done all wrong. The grandparent-grandchild relationship is <u>sacred</u>. Mama, so long as granny and granddaddy are sane and safe, get out of the way. Delicious prefers the company of Gnome and Sharky without me. I can't imagine never letting my boys spend the night with Delicious on her farm. Why on earth do some couples give up alone time when they have healthy willing relatives who will provide relief?

Granddaddy and Little Sharky

The same goes with nieces and nephews. I love my sis-in-law Dogwood Debutante, but I savor every rare moment I have alone with my nieces Balloon Girl and Cake. We have our own inside jokes and tender moments. I would be sad without that trust from Dogwood Deb. Mama, let your child get dirty. I made Sharky and Balloon Girl walk through our creek all the way from The Crippled Beagle Farm to Uncle Gravy and Aunt BBJ's farm. It was a hoot and one of my favorite memories with my sweet niece. If you set your child up to be untouchable, others will see her that way and may hesitate to interact with her. Dresses are for church and picture day. Mama, now and then, loosen your rules. One Halloween, a mother told me that she was going to let her daughter, a well-behaved pink princess, go door to door and fill her orange pumpkin with treats. But when the princess went to bed, the mama planned to throw all her candy in the trash. Say what? Boo! As soon as the mother was distracted in another conversation, I gave pitiful princess a cupcake. Oh, yes, I did. And she liked it. Oh, she liked it.

BBJ and Trout introduce Sharky to a large mouth bass.

One should not sweat in a grocery store, dressing room, or restaurant. Is a toddler tantrum tearing you down and making it tough to select the right yogurt, bra, or mixed drink? Don't make excuses, make an exit. If I take the time to drive Gnome to the farm, I dang sure don't want to sit next to your screaming meanie when I'm out on the town with Tall Child! Go to the car. Better yet, order take-out until your child can behave in a restaurant. After Sharky threw a bowl of shredded cheese across El Charro, we banned him from eating in public until age five. My love of take-out was born.

Two of my cousins actually bought a bicycle for Sharky and taught him to ride. What a great memory for them to share. My other cousins and friends are also generous with pictures on social media, which I really enjoy. If distance is an issue, send some baby swag to loving relatives and friends. I love to mail Gnome's and Sharky's sometimes impressive, sometimes disturbing schoolwork to loved ones. The recipients gain knowledge of my boys' development and typically get a laugh out of their worksheet answers. Plus, I can fill an envelope without having to actually write much.

I hate to admit this, but I think it's human nature. As a teacher, if a parent was rude to me, I had to work hard to separate the child from the parent. The child was a reminder of a negative experience, so parents, cause no negative experiences. Take good care of teachers. Don't tempt them to tag your child as obnoxious just because you are.

Don't be overwhelmed, new mother. There are lots of shortcuts available. I sneakily delegate some hard stuff. Delicious does the scrapbooks. I just mail everything to her. The first three months of his life, infant Gnome often slept in his Owl-themed bouncy seat beside me in a full-sized bed, which was beside his perfectly suitable baby bed. I loaded up on melatonin and shook right beside him until the alarm when off. Toddler Sharky spun permanent grooves into hardwood floors with his Big Wheel stunts. For the life of me, I couldn't talk a three-year-old Gnome into using the toilet. I begged, "Do you want to take your diaper off and do number two, pleeeeaaassseee?"

He said, "No way, that's disgusting." I just laughed and powdered his precious bottom. Anyone that articulate can control things when he decides to. He is nine and still can't tie his shoes. I told him, "Oh, just ask a friend." Maybe he can meet a girl that way someday.

I let my boys drink from baby bottles as long as possible because it made giving them medicine so much easier. One spring break, affluent schoolmates scattered to sun, sand, or ski slopes. Sharky said, "Mama, [so and so] is going to see the ocean tomorrow! [So and so 2] is going to California! Where are we going for spring break?"

"Nowhere."

He said, "Oh, shoot" and sulked off to his room. He was a really sweet child and I felt guilty that my poor adult decisions had put me to work and him at home on every school break. When he said "shoot," I got an idea.

I called him into the room and said, "Sharky, how about I let you cuss for spring break?" He and his friends had been daring each other, and this was the perfect and frugally fun solution. He was seven. That was probably not the best parenting move. But, as offensive as his language was (he even exhibited road rage, calling a driver a "shut-up man"), at least he offended only me, and we kept his inappropriateness private. Sunday night before school was to resume, I said, "Okay Sharky, no more cussing after tonight. Did you have a good spring break?"

"Yes ma'am."

"Wonderful. Do you want to say one more bad thing before you go night-night?"

"Yes ma'am."

"Okay, go ahead."

Sharky said, "Don't give me your honky bullsh*t, Buttermaker."

~~~

By the time Gnome is a legal adult, I'll be so old that Tall Child, Joe L., and I will be falling down a lot and fighting over the remote in our efficiency condo. If my children aren't likeable, maybe I won't actually know it. Until then, I'll do the best I can. Big girl tired. I make mistakes. I think Delicious did a good job with me. Like any well-raised girl, I throw my ugly fits at home and act perfectly polite in public. I hope my boys do too. I hope a grown Sharky never shouts, "Out of the way, shut-up man."

Full disclosure: I wrote the first draft of this Theory when my boys were really young. I revised it once. Now that Sharky and Gnome and I are older and have, um, had some life experiences, my goals are much simpler:

1. Raise children who have personal relationships with Jesus.
2. Raise children who can live independently.
3. Raise children who other people like in case said children can't live independently and need roommates.

With these sharpened goals that focus on independence, it occurs to me that my boys need to know how to behave in the workplace. They have an edge, being not women, but something is lacking. Oh! Maybe I can hustle up a summer camp for workplace etiquette. Napa Valley, I see you. I see you.

Theory 45: Workplace etiquette class should be a graduation requirement.

As I write this, my hands are crippled with cold. My house is a toasty 55 degrees, Sharky is begging to get on the computer, and dishes are piled up with no generic Cascade in sight. Gnome is roaming. I'm trapped by snow, icy roads, miserably cold temperatures, and no decent space heater. Plus, Sharky used up all the hot water in his shower so I had to take a cold shower. But, I'd rather work here in my old cold house than in any office with other humans. Why? Sometimes we working women just need a break from the scenery. We need a break from the routine. And, we need a break from the drama and stress caused by our coworkers.

As a business education career technical teacher, I did my best to enlighten the students who passed through my classes, but maybe I should hustle up this idea of workplace etiquette class for emerging and regressing adults and charge a nominal, um, fair fee. According to my sources, there is quite a need. This book could double in size if I told all the anecdotes from my banking and teaching days, much less IHOP and summer tourism work. Opportunities abound! So, what if I did create such a course? How would that look? Pretend you are reading a college catalog.

Workplace Etiquette 101 - Course Description
In Workplace Etiquette 101 students of all ages will develop the attitude and behaviors of professionalism to advance toward career goals while avoiding termination. Topics include: demonstrating appropriate dining behavior in break rooms, controlling the tongue, mastering telecommunications skills and equipment, analyzing body language, and exhibiting overall self-control when in possession of sensitive information.

Note to instructors: You must teach and assess with explicit learning outcomes. Standards are expressed in student-friendly terminology to maximize value-added growth. Standards are broken down with specific non-examples for unquestionable clarification. Standards are addressed toward females for the simplicity of using only one gender in pronouns (her/she) and because men are easier to work with than women and few men need this course. Also, the words *they*, *them*, and *their* are plural. Forever.

First, student, let's address workplace writing etiquette, also known as basic grammar and mechanics. In case a writer and her retired English teacher mother are looking for Tom's Vinegar & Salt potato chips or a restroom in your convenience store, have a coworker proofread your signs. Remember to be positive and neutral. I found these two signs on the same day. The SAME day. Are you surprised that they were in two stores about three miles apart in East Tennessee? Come on, neighbors. Underneath the photos, I attempt to translate the "writers" messages in literal terms.

1. Someone mysterious who is not named in the subject of what should be a sentence offers employment behind that door. He requires that you write in all capital letters, which means you can yell. He doesn't hire you on this side. He hires ONLY behind the door.
2. Maybe the writer misspelled *employees* and left out the predicate and punctuation. He didn't finish the sentence, so the mystery now is what employees *do* "only beyond this point" as opposed to what they do on my side of the door.

1. I despise random capitalization. Too much here. Too much.

2. *Employee's* is a possessive pronoun. I ask, "Employee's only what?" Also, it's misspelled if he intends a plural subject. Even spelled correctly as *employees'*, we infer that two or more workers own ONLY one thing or do only one thing, but we have no idea because the writer moves on to another phrase without solving the mystery of what the employee(s) only has/have or does/do.

3. *Say's*, unless it's a person's name (I don't know anyone named Say, do you?), says (ha) that Say owns the employees.

4. The homemade sign says what it says, but it doesn't indicate that we shoppers should not open that door. The homemade sign states that if you don't collect a paycheck from this store, you should never enter the store. At least the writer thanks us and adds squiggle art.

5. In this second sign, I like that the writer felt he had to elaborate in case readers couldn't understand the STANDARD "Employees Only" sign that already hangs on the door.

6. I also like that he misspelled the same word that is right above his own sign.

Delicious was with me. She said, "This is embarrassing. I guess we need to bring paper, White-Out, pens, and tape everywhere we go, Bug."

CAUTION!!! CRUCIAL!!! READ BEFORE YOU CONTINUE: I, Bug, gathered these peeves from Theories readers throughout cyberspace. These peeves are not all mine. Oh, no. Actually, I came up with a few of them because I am guilty of committing them. This Theory is not an opportunity to be offended, but an opportunity to be enlightened and improve workplace etiquette. Plus, you can print it/email it/like it/share it onward to enlighten any coworker who may benefit from such instruction.

Standard 1: Real Estate Rules

1.1 Don't touch my stuff. It is super rude to sling your nasty pocketbook up on somebody's desk. Don't you set it in the floor in the quasi-bathrooms at state parks and greasy restaurants? Gross! Plus, no one wants your Black Lab tendrils all over her perfect lab reports. Also, don't set a dripping drink on her day planner. She may be neurotic, but your dollar sweet tea could cause her to miss a meeting, a conference call, or the one-hour online flash sale she's hitting during said conference call.

1.2 Get off her turf. If you want to see what your coworker is up to on the computer, friend her. Don't look over her shoulder. What if she's writing a letter of resignation, checking her bank balance, or ate boiled eggs for lunch? You sure you want to take that risk? Back up.

1.3 Know the zones. *General workers:* Don't let customers behind the desk/line/counter/employee door, especially if you wait tables. Once a customer has seen the restaurant kitchen, she is never the same, and the food tastes different. *Teachers:* NEVER send students to the teacher's lounge/break room/copy room. Ever. They might hear some Common [Core] language they aren't mature enough to handle.

1.4 Don't walk into an office or classroom and comment on what you observe unless you have something positive to say. Yes, my students were loud because I was loud. And they were happy. And my class was more fun than your Honors English I. Thank goodness someone loaned me the phrase "buzz of learning." Yes, that's what you heard, you old grouchy teachers. My students weren't gossiping, vaping under the tables, putting 6,000 dragon images in the shared network folder, or planning weekend parties. What you heard was the "buzz of learning" from their excitement over an Excel lesson!

Standard 2: Use furniture, fixtures, and equipment the right way or don't use them at all.

2.1 Printers are off limits! If you need your coworker's granny's banana pudding recipe, ask nicely and she'll print you a copy. Don't just show up in her room and start jerking Christmas cards out of her tray.

2.2 Don't abuse the copier. Manuals are online for a reason, but some of us do need paper for note taking and analysis. Plus, some of us can't figure out how to find those online manuals in the first place. Everyone else, back off the toner. Walgreens and Snapfish are great places to order your wedding invitations. Teachers, throw the ditto up on your Smart Board. Don't Xerox and waste thousands of copies and every other teacher's planning period by hogging the copier.

2.3 If you jam the copier, own up to it. Suck it up and call the number on the sticker. When you leave the copy room with the "original document" and nothing else, we know. We. All. Know.

2.4 Everyone should communicate on the same horizontal plane. When you set up your office, make sure the chairs or couch in front of your desk are the same height as your chair. When coworkers, employees, or interviewees come in and sit down, they should look AT you not UP at you. Just because you are "higher up" doesn't mean you have to literally be higher up.

2.5 Don't abuse the break room.
If you are on a high protein, low carb diet, eat bacon and cheese. It is not cool to heat left over cabbage in the common microwave.

2.6 Pack your own snacks. It is unsanitary to eat from a coworker's plate or from the trash can. Also, chew with your mouth closed.

2.7 Everyone deserves a key to the building. Student teachers and trainees and branch managers and new hires of any kind should not have to wait and dive through a door when an actual keyholder enters with his fancy striped keycard.

Standard 3: Respect coworkers' time. Time means money. Extra time means sanity. Personal time is personal.

3.1 If you walk into a coworker's classroom or office and she's on the phone, turn around. Don't stare her down. Once, I was on the phone with my cousin Bags during the workday. We were laughing it up when Bags sighed, "Ugh, Bug, I have to hang up. There's a mouth breather staring at me through the glass. It's getting foggy. I have to go."

3.2 Don't ask an employee to go to the grocery store for work, after work. If you need supplies, give her the money for items *and* gas up front and send her during work hours, not on her own time.

3.3 Be on time for everything all the time. Or be early. Red Hot can hit two school zones, by a sausage biscuit, and acquire a large

Starbucks and still get to work on time. So can you. Flat-tired teachers are always getting rides from each other, and they make it on time. So can you.

3.4 Cancel all birthdays and baby showers. In the workplace, why do WOMEN do this to each other? I'm glad you are fertile, but that does not mean I want to extend my workday. Men don't charge each other $25 per child or birthday. Ever. If you are in a new company, don't set a precedent for these expensive, inconvenience, annoying forced social situations. Don't shame your colleague who doesn't attend. Maybe being at a bridal shower or baby shower causes her heartache. Maybe she needs money for her own husband and baby. Maybe she just wants to go the hell home. See Standard 3.2.

3.5 Don't ask an employee to sell Visa credit cards, in other words, WORK, while on vacation. True story. My boss asked me to take Visa card applications on my vacation to Panama City Beach. He said, "We have branches there. You could go up to people while you are hanging out by the ocean and ask if them to apply." Really? Who wants to be accosted by a tipsy mama in a swimsuit toting a clipboard of credit card brochures and a Paper Mate pen? I refused. He wrote me up for being insubordinate. As Ramses said in *The Ten Commandments*, "So let it be written, so let it be done."

Standard 4: Don't be a techno-snob.

4.1 Sometimes paper is better. You may zip through commands on your MAC at home, but the 70-year-old loan officer who says "hunt and poke" is just as efficient on paper. Don't judge. To spell is to spell, no matter the medium. I force tutoring clients to use the real dictionary. Ah, simple fun at a teenager's expense. Stop telling me about apps. Ugh.

4.2 Train for success. If your coworker moves the mouse, checks the screen to see where it went, moves the mouse again, checks the screen again, etc., gently offer a lesson or do the regulatory exam for her. SEC/FDIC/OSHA officials, for your information, no one over 65 takes those tests. Their 30-year-old bosses do the tests for them. Stop wasting everyone's time. Maybe I should Tweet Trump and ask him to direct the federal organizations to chill out on computer-based-training. I know he would agree with me.

4.3 All supplies matter. If your coworker is old school and needs White-Out and mechanical pencils, order them. Sometimes, I slap a ruler against my computer screen. I am not ashamed.

4.4 Apply operating system skills to written communication. Emails should be no longer than one paragraph. Stop with the essays and attachments. Write with positive and neutral phrases. Remember, you are competing with Old Navy and Groupon.

Standard 5: Practice and interpret appropriate verbal and non-verbal communication strategies.

5.1 Master the art of workplace storytelling. Record the length, time, and date of your stories so you don't repeat them more than once a month. I hereby apologize to everyone with whom I've ever worked.

5.2 Tit for tat. If you tell stories, don't act annoyed and too busy to listen when you have to hear a story. Again. This week.

5.3 Let sleeping dogs lie until a customer shows up. If you have an employee/coworker who sleeps, call her when the customer is about twenty feet away. That will give her time to sit up and wipe the drool off her chin. Oh, and don't text a coworker while drinking. You'll unintentionally promise to go to her mother's Avon party on Friday. You will not want to go.

5.4 Make eye contact.

5.5 Demonstrate phone call consideration. Really? Don't text at 3:30 a.m. because the recipient may wake up and text back at 3:38 a.m. Snow days are like lottery-won vacation days. Keep them sacred.

5.6 Don't interrupt. For teachers specifically: If a fellow teacher is talking to you, don't interrupt her story to tell students to be quiet.

She may be having a romantic crisis. She needs you. Interrupting her means you aren't listening in the first place. So rude. Let students enjoy the buzz of learning while you help her sort out life.

5.7 Smile. Don't walk around with a constant frown on your face. At least *look* happy. I tried to impress this through an essay by saying it takes more muscles to frown than smile. Fortunately, I did the research. It actually takes more muscles to smile. Work that out.

5.8 Demonstrate polite behavior. If you are walking down the hall and someone passes, look up, make eye contact, and SPEAK.

5.9 Stop your whining. You work to make money. You are paid to work. Be positive. Don't complain when someone trusts you with more work. Do it and be thankful.

5.9 Operate efficiently on the dreaded conference call. Who came up with these? Don't be that chic who chimes in, states her name a couple of times, and touts some numbers just to be obviously present. We all know you are in the dressing room at Belk Department Store.

Standard 6: Watch your mouth. Watch your hands.

6.1 Don't suck up to the boss. It's obvious. We all see it. You are embarrassing yourself. There is no way in helk you live in the south and are a fan of curling.

6.2 Stay out of the lounge if you are weak. Gossip and negativity are bad, even though everything you hear is 100 percent accurate.

6.3 Keep romantic stories out of the office, especially if they take place *in* the office. Exclusion is cruel. If something truly is going on, and you know about it, share every detail so no one feels left out.

6.4 Be prepared to combat come-ons. Borrow one from Bug: A coworker invited me to skinny dip in his pool one night when his wife was out of town. I remarked, "It's tempting because I've always wondered if my stretch marks glow in the dark."

These days, I have limited work etiquette issues. I speak freely, type whatever I want to, and I book client appointments only on bra days. My routine begins with coffee, the Holy Bible, the *Harbrace Handbook*, and a to-do list on paper. Once I take Gnome to UE and usher Sharky off to high school, I grind through one sentence at a time for my clients and me. Phone calls are uninterrupted because my only coworker is the snoozing calico cat Lollipop. She sits under my desk lamp and judges me, but she does so silently. She can't call human resources. We interact, but only when my hands get cold. Lolli is great at warming them. I pick her up, rub her soft fur, and give her a kiss. When I tried that with human colleagues, it didn't go so well.

Reader, thank you for spending time with me. I hope you found a friend on every page!

Find all my work on Amazon and Kindle, through my website, www.jodydyer.com, or in person/by order at a variety of retail stores. To book me for an event, send an email or use the contact form on the website.

If you'd like to be part of my research for future books, friend or follow me on social media. I frequently ask readers for input.

Interested in telling your own story? I am a writing coach, ghostwriter, editor, and boutique publisher, and I embrace the opportunity to help others tell their stories. Remember, I taught middle school. I can work with anyone.

Email: dyer.cbpublishing@gmail.com
Website: www.jodydyer.com
On Facebook: *Author Jody Dyer* and *Crippled Beagle Publishing*

Other titles:

Theories: Size 12, Laugh! You know you want to.

The Eye of Adoption: A Turbulent True Story of Heartache, Humor, & Hope

Field Day (for children)

Parents, Stop and Think

#beyondwords

Perspectives, An Anthology of Original Works by Pellissippi State Community College Creative Writing Club

Made in the USA
Coppell, TX
27 November 2019